Cross-Cultural
Management

Cross-Cultural Management

Veronica Velo

Cross-Cultural Management

First published in 2011 by
Business Expert Press, LLC
222 East 46th Street, New York, NY 10017
www.businessexpertpress.com

ISBN-13: 978-1-60649-350-2 (paperback)

ISBN-13: 978-1-60649-351-9 (e-book)

DOI 10.4128/9781606493519

A publication in the Business Expert Press Human Resource Management and Organizational Behavior Collection

Collection ISSN: 1946-5637 (print)
Collection ISSN: 1946-5645 (electronic)

Cover design by Jonathan Pennell
Interior design by Exeter Premedia Services Private Ltd., Chennai, India

First edition: 2011

10 9 8 7 6 5 4 3 2 1

Printed in the United States of America.

I would like to dedicate this book to P. J. Sheahan
and to G. Macedra

Abstract

The book offers an introduction to cross-cultural management through an exploration of the major theories that have been developed in the fields of business anthropology and international management. An introduction to the concept of culture is followed in subsequent chapters by a comparative description of different typologies which will be used to explain various expected behaviors in intercultural business settings.

The fundamental issues in cross-cultural management are also discussed, namely What is culture? How can we describe it? To what extent is it important in international business? And we introduce the main frameworks used in the discipline to identify and analyze cultural differences.

In the second part of the book, we introduce the reader to the main frameworks discussed in Part I and to real-life, cross-cultural situations in the business environment. We introduce discussions on the application of previously analyzed cultural frameworks as a basis for the elaboration of new ideas relating to current issues in organizational behavior. International organizations normally deal with topics such as the relationships between the employee as a socialized individual and the culture of his/her organization, managing in a globalized context, the development and management of cross-cultural teams, negotiating interculturally and dealing with subsequent potential conflicts, and so forth.

The final part of the book part elaborates on how the globalized economy projects its needs for inclusion and understanding. From the ethics perspective, we describe the need to find a coherent pattern of norms that are widely accepted and shared in spite of diversity, and how to define and act under the paradox of equality in spite of differences.

Keywords

intercultural management, cross-cultural management, globalization, international business, international behavior, intercultural behavior, international business negotiations, intercultural conflict

Contents

Preface

The aim of this book is simple, although I would have preferred it to be something more than simple.

Perhaps it may sound pompous to say that I aim to contribute to the understanding of people and to make people happier in the workplace. But it is true. This is what I would like this book to accomplish.

My generation has not been educated to be international, to think inter-culturally, to be citizens of the world. At most, some of us have been brought up to be binational if circumstances compelled us. But in general we learned at school our national anthem and the glories of our ancestors much earlier than we were invited to discover with curiosity the mysteries of alternative ways of thinking, perceiving, and feeling... at home and abroad.

Geert Hofstede, the greatest author in terms of cultural anthropology (in my humble view) has written on his weblog, *"Culture is more often a source of conflict than of synergy. Cultural differences are a nuisance at best and often a disaster"* (http://www.geert-hofstede.com/). I must admit that I felt very sad when I read this statement, because unfortunately I feel this is true. I would not like cultures to be a nuisance or a disaster, but rather a source of creativity and continuous challenge to the boundaries of our thought. I would love cultures to be the source of inspiration and understanding.

Honestly, I am not sure this book will help me change the world over-night. But at least I hope it will give the readers a few hints on how to work better with others and use diversity as an asset, not as a barrier to overcome.

The book's structure is very simple. First, I will present a model that will help us understand why we think differently, why we assume differ-ently, and why we act differently in different cultures. Then I will review the most commonly discussed frameworks for cultural analysis to see how these differences operate in our ways of thinking and feeling. And finally I will explore applications of these differences in business situations.

This book has "exercises" at the end of each chapter. I am using quo-tations marks for the word "exercises" because I am not sure this is what they are. Very honestly, I would prefer to call them "invitations to have readers think on specific points elaborated in this chapter," because I am not sure whether there are right or wrong answers to them. And to be honest... who am I to think there are any right or wrong answers in anything relating to cross-cultural management? Even more than in theoretical physics, in cross-cultural management, "Everything is relative, Dr. Einstein." What is really important is to have people challenge themselves and assume there might be alternative ways of perceiving reality. If my questions succeed in doing that, then it will be wonderful.

Nevertheless, let me suggest an approach you may find useful to tackle these "invitations to think." Ideally, the most important thing would be to face the activity suggestions with an open mind and try to solve the puzzles relating them to situations you have faced in the past and think what you could have done better. Try to focus on the things that went wrong and find the origin of these misunderstandings, misapprehensions, misconceptions, miscommunications, and so forth. But do not feel regret, just think how you could do better next time.

If you have never been in such a situation in the past, try asking for help from someone who has, or could have been in a similar situation; get into chat rooms dealing with the topics in hand, find people from the cultures in question, and discuss points of views with them.

But if you have any questions or would like to discuss any particular topic further, I am at your disposal. My email is veronica@veronicavelo.com. I will not promise to answer all and each of the questions appearing in the book individually for every single reader who writes to me, but I am open to listening to your suggestions or questions and getting back to you on them. My consultancy group also prepares seminars in cross-cultural management for people willing to take matters further.

I am not sure readers of this book will feel as strongly as I do the need to investigate with passion the unknown in others or the deep curiosity to explore the reasons for their behavior and attitudes. But I would have done a good job if some of you readers think "Oh, that is why!" or "Oh, that is what happened really!" when going through these pages.

In any case, I hope this book will be useful and that a few years from now, when upcoming generations will have realized that living and working with others is much more fun when we understand them than when we judge them, they will find my writings still useful and relevant.

In the meantime, enjoy your reading...

Acknowledgments

I would like to thank Greg Bissky, Ming Li, Sophie Hennekam, and Andrew Barron for their contributions to chapters 4, 6, 9, and 11, respectively.

PART I

Introduction to Cross-Cultural Management

CHAPTER 1

Introduction to Cross-Cultural Management

Contextualizing Background Information

Globalization has probably developed faster than our capacity to "digest" all the changes it involves. One of the most stunning revelations that accompany globalization is the notion that geographical distance has changed, and with it, the way business is done.

Although globalization was estimated to have only limited effects, this is simply not the case any longer. Businesses that aim to remain mononational would simply lose too many competitive advantages to survive in any market. This obvious reality, no matter how hard to swallow for some, has been dealt with by technology quite efficiently. But the main aspects that could determine whether a business of any size would survive or die are relationships and communication: technology being an asset that is available to all players at the same level, the main competitive success factors remain (1) innovation and (2) the capacity to develop, entertain, and maintain business across borders.

Those who manage to gain the latter will probably win over those who do not, and to profit from that extra mile, the understanding of other cultures and their dynamics becomes crucial.

Many authors have tried to define what culture is and how it develops. The most commonly used definitions have originated in varied social sciences including psychology, sociology, and anthropology.

Some of these definitions include Sigmund Freud's "Culture is a construction that hides the pulsional and libido-oriented reality," Herder's "Every nation has a particular way of being and that is their culture," Kardurer's "Culture is the psycho characteristic configuration of the basis of the personality," and Sapir's "Culture is a system of behaviours that result from the socialisation process." Most of these definitions have in common the relationship between the individual and the society (s)he belongs to, and point to the "cultural" factor as being the key element of the dynamics that enhances the rapport between the two.

The notion of culture had not been thoroughly explored (or at least the concept had been not thoroughly disseminated) in management science until the 1970s. It was only in the 1980s that Dutch researcher Geert Hofstede wrote about business anthropology for the first time in his book *Culture's Consequences*,[1] which opened the door to a new discipline that studied the impact of cultural diversity on business.

Since Geert Hofstede's initial work, much has taken place in terms of updating of his data and applying it to the study of cross-cultural management. The most famous one is probably the Global Learning and Observations to Benefit the Environment (GLOBE) study, which included research on 62 societies and their approaches to leadership.[2] Similar updates have been published, but not many have included a significant number of countries.

Hofstede's definition of culture, which is certainly the most widely considered by both academics and practitioners in the management arena, states that:

> Culture is the *mental programming* of the human spirit that allows distinguishing the members of one category in comparison with the members of another category. It is the conditioning that we share with the other members of the same group.

The key word in Hofstede's definition of culture is certainly "mental programming." It appears as both the link that "glues" all members of a group through a common set of assumptions and the behaviors resulting from them. At the same time, this collective similarity defines members by the exclusion of those who do not share the same background, and signs and symbols are therefore designed to exteriorize and, if possible, make visible who is part of which category and who is not.

Mental programming is a learnt attitude to life and a set of expected behaviors that could easily lead to stereotyping, as a safety net produced by society, to avoid the expected delusion that could naturally lead to frustration in having to face reactions that do not match with what is supposed to be "the natural way of acting and feeling" according to what the reference group has taught its members since their early childhood.

The Notion of Mental Programming

Geert Hofstede, who as mentioned above could be considered the father of business anthropology, has developed the concept of "mental programming." Mental programming is what makes us expect a certain type of behavior from others. Any other action or reaction will be interpreted in varied ways, from "weird" to "shocking." Interpretations of the same behavior may differ and vary from culture to culture.

For example, if I am from a culture where the boss has to show authority at all times and his/her decisions are not to be contested or even questioned by subordinates, then my mental programming will make me surprised when confronted with a situation in which a trainee openly objects to a comment made by the Director General in a meeting in front of all the other employees. Perhaps, in a different culture the same behavior would be interpreted as extreme interest, enthusiasm, and willingness to contribute, as expressed by the trainee.

Mental programming has to do with the glass through which we see life. We understand other people's behavior (or we fail to understand it) according to the perspective from which we explore their attitudes and actions, and these viewpoints are strongly hardwired in the notions we have incepted through the socialization process.

In social sciences' jargon, the word "socialization" refers to the process through which one learns the basic notions of "good," "bad," "acceptable," "non-acceptable," "okay," and "not okay." Social learning (or socialization) does not occur in a formal manner, but in an informal way, through experience and trial and error. When a mother suggests to her female children that they ought to learn how to do the cleaning and the washing at home, whereas their brothers are dispensed from that task, little girls learn that they are expected to assume a social role later on in life that is more connected to the care and service of their families, rather than with what is considered as "male activities" (the activities the boys of their age are expected to perform).

We are socialized by what our parents tell us, also by how they talk to us, how they react to others, and in particular by how they react to us, according to whether they consider our own behavior to be acceptable or not. Showing emotions in public, for example, can be considered as acceptable and even desirable in Southern European cultures, as it is commonly considered that those who are "poker faced" are not to be trusted. On the other hand, in Scandinavian cultures, not being able to control your emotions is perceived to be a sign of immaturity and related behaviors can be punished by a generalized shunning of the person exposing them.

However, parents are by far not the only socialization factor. Equally important are school, TV programs, and the media, which teach us what is correct or incorrect, normal or abnormal, acceptable or unacceptable. For instance, since the mid-2000s, European TV has made efforts to show representatives of minorities. Suddenly, weather presenters were not exclusively White and Asian, Latino, and Black Bond girls invaded the cinema screens in an attempt to generate a larger inclusion of previously neglected minority groups, who had been subconsciously receiving the message that "only white people are nice and showable on TV" and "Bond girls are usually blond", and therefore may have understood "I can never be fully included in this society, which is basically not designed for people like me."

Socialization can therefore be defined as a means to learn how to behave in a particular society, and is a basic element of our mental programming, which is the link that defines our belonging to a culture by the exclusion of those who do not share it.

The Facebook trail below illustrates a real-life case of cultural misunderstanding experienced by a British traveler (Stephen Gabbutt), on a business trip to Italy with his family, and the reactions of some of his compatriots (a few, a bit fueled by the author of this book).

Stephen Gabbutt   None of the horde of Italian kids on today's BA flight have sat in the right seats, so none of the Brit families and couples can sit together, classic Italianess. Can we go now?

Veronica Velo   Get culturally sensitive by kicking those kids' arses. Latin parents (whether they are Latin American or Latin European) tend to outsource to strangers the setting of limits to their children because they fear the loss of their love. Too much

Francoise Dolto in their readings, see?... Actually, my cousins' children usually refer to me as "the ugly witch who lives by a scary Castle in Europe".

July 25 at 1:02 pm · LikeUnlike · 1 person *Ged Casey likes this.*

Candice Hart   Give the ex lax and pretend it's chocolate and when they pooping their pants outside the toilet you can steal their seats.

July 25 at 1:36 pm · UnlikeLike · 1 person *Loading...*

Alison Clark   Its probably BAs fantastic seat allocation system. We were on a flight to Paris once and had to sit behind each other, as did another couple near us. Hope you found a quiet corner!

July 25 at 2:01 pm · LikeUnlike

Stephen Gabbutt   Thanks for the comments Ladies, just seeing a load of pooped British BA customers trying to explain to 11 year old Italians that they where sitting in their seat using hand gestures and pointing at their tickets was priceless. I'm sorry to say Lady V I don't do culturally sensitive and it just makes me shout loader and point more.

July 25 at 5:50 pm · LikeUnlike

Veronica Velo   I am about to start up a birth control campaign just to piss the Pope off. Will you travel to Rome with me in order to distribute free condoms? It sounds like a long term solution...

July 25 at 6:00 pm · LikeUnlike

Veronica Velo   Why did you not ask the BA onboard crew for assistance? They should have replaced all the children in the right seats, shouldn't they?

July 26 at 10:29 pm · LikeUnlike

Stephen Gabbutt   They tried, but many of the single travelling business blokes just sat somewhere else to save the time.

Wednesday at 8:02 am · LikeUnlike

In the above dialog, we can distinguish some of the elements that constitute the stereotypical British mental programming, as opposed to the Italian one.

In Italy, the general assumption is that rules can be slightly (at least) broken. Rules are imperfect, and they are not universal. They need, therefore, to be adapted to each situation. Rules such as seating arrangements may be seen as a formality that can be disregarded if other options are available that cause no discomfort to anyone (as rules do not necessarily derive from rationality, but perhaps from the need of the President of the Airline to reinforce his power through the imposition of aleatory norms). In this case, the fact of having children sit anywhere was not perceived as a disruption, but as a slight alteration to the rules that would make the children as happy as their parents (who would manage to get rid of them for a while). This behavior may have bothered the British passengers, but as ties with them were not expected to last for longer than 2 hours, there was not much point in trying to please them.

On the other hand, relationships between Italian parents and their children are meant to last for life. Children in Italy have traditionally been considered as those who will take care of their parents in their old age (perhaps as a payback to their parents, for having taken care of them when they were young), and therefore are spoiled much more than British children. Italian children, have traditionally played the Social Security role for parents in their old age, and therefore the emotional links between them have developed in different ways than in the United Kingdom.

In the British mindset, on the other hand, rules are supposed to be the result of thorough thought on what would be the best way to ensure the common good (in this case, a pleasant flight for everyone). And as long as rules are clearly communicated, it is everyone's duty to abide by them. Failure to do so can be considered as a sign of rudeness or disrespect toward those who have to suffer from the consequences of such actions. Also, children are expected to behave, and it is their parents' duty to make sure that they learn not to disturb others. The behavior of children is supposed to be the responsibility of their parents.

In such a context, the sources of conflict are multiple, as are the reactions from each party, directly deriving from their different mental programming, which is interestingly incompatible.

For instance, the Italians would have expected the British adults to talk to the children directly and have them move from the seats they were occupying without caring much about whether the children would find other seats or not (they probably would not have, as the single business-men were occupying them at the time). By doing so, the conflict would have been smaller (there is usually no conflict because the Italian children would probably have moved when told to do so by an adult) and then the Italian parents would have assumed the charge of making arrangements with the businessmen.

It is worthwhile noticing that the notion of time and its use is very different across cultures. A British person would have considered a delay in the flight as something much more serious than an Italian (who would probably have considered it as part of the fun of traveling), and there-fore the Italian parents would not have taken into consideration the extra time involved in rearranging the seating once, and if, the British had complained.

The reaction of the British was also quite strange to the Italians. Why would they just present the problem *after* a solution had been found? The Italian parents must have felt quite surprised that the British parents confronted them at the arrival airport. If they were so angry about the change in seating, why had they not said so before? And actually, why were they so angry, instead of being grateful for having been given the glorious chance of relaxing out of the way of the misbehavior of their children for a while? For the Italians, the fact that the British did not complain before or during the flight meant that the slight change in rules did not actually bother them so much. For the British, it meant that there was no point in delaying a flight for a quarrel, but that the point had to be made regarding the situation in order to re-establish a sense of justice.

It is also interesting to note the comments of the British Facebook friends. Some tried to be polite and funny about the situation, suggesting a revenge for the "affront" at least equivalent in strength: "the poisoning of the children" (this was obviously a joke, but the interesting part is that there was the assumption that the Italians had *meant* to bother them and therefore ought to be punished for that). In a culture in which conflict and expression of emotions are to be minimized in order to ensure harmony and the continuing of social processes with minimum disruption, a quiet payback allowing to "set the accounts right" appears to be the most civi-lized option. Interestingly enough, for the Italians, having a British adult telling their children off would not have shocked anyone and would have appeared as a simple act of civilization for which they might even have been grateful, as it would have contributed to the general education of their little ones. On the other hand, any sort of quiet revenge would have led them to think of the British as "those poker-faced people who stab you in the back" (to remain within the same tone of funny exaggeration).

Other British comments blamed the procedures, probably because according to those making the comments, a good system cannot fail. Failure occurs out of the system, not out of people in it. In other words, if the Italians did not end up in the assigned seats, it must have been because the seating arrangement was wrong. In no (British) mind would it be normal to think that any civilized individual would simply ignore British Airways policy. Besides, such a statement was an attempt to show the open-mindedness of the poster, as the assumption was that it was all part of a professional mistake, nothing to do with Italian "lack of consideration." The Facebook friend in this case just failed to ignore that what could be considered as an act of disrespect in a British mindset would not be so in an Italian one, and vice-versa, as in an Italian mind making a fuss about a seat during a relatively short flight was just a sign of excessive rigidity and lack of flexibility, which showed no attempt to develop peaceful relations with passengers from another country (the height of impoliteness and lack of civility in an Italian mind).

Interestingly enough, the "victim" in this anecdote gave up. He was frustrated, but surrendered to the fact that there would have been no way to communicate with the other party. He just gave up, obviously due to the language barrier to start with, but also knowing that the misunderstanding would be rooted deeper than that. His unwillingness to make an effort was probably partly based on his exasperation when thinking that it would be up to *him* to go against his own mental programming by "acting Italian" (i.e., doing what no British person would do, like telling a stranger's child off) or educating the Italians on his own mental programming (i.e., in Britain, telling someone else's child off is worse than telling the parents off, not only because it can be considered abuse, but also because it suggests the parents are unable to assume their social role as educators).

My own first reaction to the scenes presented was to suggest that Italians should stop existing, as their very existence in the world would bother the British (always pushing on the very British joking style of communication), to which there was no immediate response. Anything expressed in that sense could have been considered rude, impolite, or—even worse—racist, and that would be definitely not British at all.

So, if you were British and you were in a similar situation, what would you have done? Below is my humble suggestion.

Veronica Velo	If I were you, I would write a complaint letter to BA because it is part of their job to make sure that logistics run smoothly. Also, remember that and part of what you paid over what you would have paid to travel with Ryanair or other cheap airlines was supposed to be justified by the fact you could sit next to your family. So they owed that to you as a company. By the way, if you could include my business card in your letter and suggest BA buys some of my training on how to avoid this sort of problems in the future, I would be grateful... (and you would get a commission, of course!)

Wednesday at 10:18 am · LikeUnlike

Veronica Velo	I am using this trail in my book. You are not allowed to sue me for plagiarism and you will touch no royalties, though.

a few seconds ago · LikeUnlike

Challenging one's own mental programming requires much energy. It demands almost more energy than learning a new language, because it implies assuming that everything one knows *for sure* may be wrong in another context, and this can be destabilizing.

How insecure can one feel if suddenly everything that was an absolute truth became ambiguous or uncertain, or even easily challenged by others who have a different absolute truth they stand by?

Many have chosen to bomb those with different ideas, to eradicate them from the surface of the Earth, and others have even concocted plans to make them disappear or simply kick them out of their countries. For those following these ideas, this book and the understanding of the concept of culture is of no use.

On the other hand, if the aim is to do business with people who come to the negotiating table or to work as a team with those who have a different mindset, then the challenge is on, and knowing as much as possible about their feelings and thoughts (basically where they are coming from) can help simply because the understanding of mental programming is all that it is about.

An old Chinese parable recounts the tale of a few blind men trying to describe what an elephant is. As they cannot see, each one of them is touching a different part of the animal and making attempts to describe what it is like based on their tactile impressions. The one touching the eye says, "an elephant is a round, wet surface," to which the one holding the tail responds "not at all, an elephant is like a rope," and the third one, touching the leg, says, "an elephant is like a vertical tube, with a nail at the bottom." Obviously all men are right, but their truth is only partial. It is only through dialog and willingness to talk to each other that they can reach a "universal" truth, if ever. When facing similar situations, the question is whether it is best to challenge one's mental programming (accept that what seems obvious to us may only be relatively true and accept other points of view, no matter how annoying, inconvenient, or ridiculous these could be) or simply reject these and remain stuck to one's convictions based on social standards.

Mental programming, no matter how constraining, is nevertheless not useless. It allows us to "get a grip" of what the world could be like at first sight and it helps us understand at least part of the reality that surrounds us, and this is crucial for us as social beings. When going international, although facing other mental programming and encountering other sets of assumptions becomes inevitable, a more complex viewpoint is required, an international one; that of a person who is ready to admit that s(he) may be considering the elephant from a relative perspective, not just out of politeness, but out of conviction.

Mental programming exists at three levels: individual, collective, and universal (Figure 1.1).[3] Individual mental programming includes all the preconceptions and structures that each one of us has developed as a result of our own personal experiences and exposure to different environments. Collective mental programming is shared by a particular group, which perceives reality in their own specific way. Universal mental programming contains all structures of thought that are shared by humans.

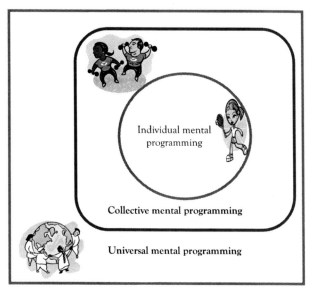

Figure 1.1. Levels of mental programming.

- An example of individual mental programming: I only buy and use handbags with many divisions because they allow me to keep my belongings in order and to easily access my diary while I am talking over the mobile phone.
- An example of collective mental programming: Women from certain cultures may expect men to pay for the bill at the restaurant, as it could be considered courteous for women to pay only when there are no men at the table.
- An example of universal mental programming: eating regularly.

When dealing with counterparts from different countries at a superficial level, we might reduce our interactions to levels that hardly exceed the level of universal mental programming, or perhaps just touch collective mental programming relating to specific generic groups that all the people concerned belong to anyway (a professional group following routine rules, a diplomatic team acting under the same protocol, etc.). These interactions can take place at a formal or informal level, but the knowledge of the parties concerned and the sharing of their lives remains vague and superficial.

Conflict or culture shock will appear when collective mental programmings interact and assumptions are not the same, leading to unfulfilled expectations and behavior considered as weird. At a personal level, mental programming becomes individual, and therefore the surprises to be processed are the same, whichever culture or social group the individuals concerned may belong to.

Values

The main component of mental programming is *values*. Values are a tendency to prefer one situation to another. A person believes in a value if he or she firmly thinks that a way of behaving is better than all others, and this, for either personal or social reasons. Values are key components of individual, collective, and universal mental programming.

The following example illustrates how values affect mental programming and how a "clash" of mental programmings can affect business relations. Khalid M. Al-Aiban and J. L. Pearce conducted a study called "The influence of values on management practices,"[4] in which they demonstrated that:

1. Managers in Saudi Arabia allocate rights and responsibilities to citizens who represent their families according to both the family's social rank and their personal status in society. Positions are then obtained through a mix of both individual merit and family position.
2. Managers in the United States allocate rights, responsibilities, and give promotions to employees mainly according to their merit.
3. Differences between the national samples have revealed them to be *cultural*. It is not that Saudi Arabian managers are unable to understand managerial practices that are commonly applied in the United States. These managers do not apply them because they are incompatible with their values.

Our values affect almost every decision we make. Dealing with people who hold different values can be irritating and exhausting, but in most cases competitive advantage is gained by those who manage to understand the dynamics of intervalue deal making over those who decide to give up. Markets can be gained, opportunities tackled, and profitable partnerships sealed, if certain openness is shown toward the fact that values can differ cross-culturally.

Values are emotional by definition, and the fact that they are not rooted in rationality may contribute to the frustration of doing business across borders. Indeed, values determine our subjective definition of rationality, or at the very least of common sense, as values are in most cases the result of personal experiences or of rules imposed on us for longer than we can remember.

Values in our minds are organized through systems of hierarchies: they are more or less important to us than other values. Conflict usually arises (even intraculturally) when two parties having contradictory values, and feel very intensively about them, interact. In cases where values are contradictory, but the intensity of the emotions toward these values by one or more of the parties involved is relatively low, concessions can take place. In the example above, if the American businessmen stick to their main value (performance) and the Saudi counterparts remain inflexible with regard to their seniority tradition, then no interactions will take place. At least one of the parties will have to make concessions for the deal to be concluded and the feasibility of that will greatly depend on how attached each one of the parties is to its own cultural values.

Another characteristic of values is that there is a difference between those that are desired and those that are desirable. Desired values are pragmatic and those espousing them take them into practice. Desirable values are those we believe in and ethically support, but we do not act upon. An example of a desired value could be that there are equal opportunities in recruitment for as long as a policy is put in place to support this value and it is reinforced. This same value becomes "desirable" if nothing is done to make sure there is equality in the workplace, no matter how strongly it is believed that this is how things should actually work. Needless to say, when two parties with contradictory values intend to make a deal, the level of ideology attached to them will determine the readiness of the parties to make concessions and therefore the likelihood of the deal being closed.

Subcultures

In general jargon, when the word "culture" is mentioned, reference is being made to the national culture or to the culture of a particular group that is set up in a specific geographic zone. Nevertheless, groups of people sharing values and mental programming can be constituted across borders and the links developed among them and across them can be as solid as those established by national links. These non-national cultures are called subcultures and they can group students studying or having studied at the same school, members of an extended family, members of the same profession or generation, individuals with the same sexual preferences, and, of course, people working for the same company.

The particular subculture that reunites people working for the same company is called corporate culture. People belonging to the same subculture develop similar sets of values and practices. In the specific case of corporate culture, these values and practices are usually reflected in the image the organization projects externally. Even though many authors including Geert Hofstede have questioned the very existence of corporate culture (the debate will be developed in chapter 5), practices shared by people acting in favor of a common institution generate a sense of commonality that reassembles them and produces a shared impression of belonging, which corresponds with that of the national culture.

Subcultures can be artificially created, like alumni associations, aiming to facilitate exchanges between selected members for the sake of a particular goal, through the achievement of compatible objectives; they can be naturally created, like that of people from the same generation; they sometimes require a specific meeting point to develop their rites and rituals, for example, Muslim believers traveling to Mecca; or they can reunite those identifying themselves with them online.

Belonging to a subculture makes communication easy, as codes, symbols, and interests are usually shared with others attached to the same group. The role of national cultures is similar to that of subcultures, in the sense that it reunites and provides a sense of identity by the exclusion of nonmembers.

Culture Stability and Cultural Change

Societies and subsocieties (cultures and subcultures) create and recreate norms of behavior and rules based on what is perceived as necessary to establish a good basis for growth and development and to ensure its own preservation.

People developing in closeness have to face similar problems and agree on joint actions to be executed, which aim to solve day-to-day or specific situations in an effective manner.

Let us consider an example. Say that a certain population has developed in an area where resources are rare and living conditions are extremely tough. This society will develop survival mechanisms that will be different from those existing in an area where resources are abundant. Habits will soon be formalized into norms and systems of rules, which will in time become the basis for the local legislation. After time, the practice of these legal precepts will be reinforced by experience and a shared notion of what is acceptable and what is not will be intersubjectively shared, creating a new and common mental programming. All social institutions are based on shared ideas of what is good and what is not so good for the society, and having established them to survive these same institutions are constantly reinforced by the same established patterns of convictions and shared ideology.

Cultures, therefore, tend to be stable, as they are the result of a series of attempts to respond and adapt to a particular environment. For as long as this response or series of responses to the environment work well, there is no need for change, perhaps other than a few alterations or small improvements that allow a most suitable adaptation.

The same pattern occurs in companies or in any other subculture. Let us consider a real-life example: furniture company IKEA. Among this company's values, one could state creativity, fast reaction to environment, and teamwork. These values and system of values were the key success factors for the company's business model and have ensured its progress through the years.

In order to reinforce these values, organizational systems and structures are created: recruitment and promotion systems, patterns like business cards that do not show the position of the employee within the company, a very flat organizational chart, and so forth.

The structures are supported by "norms" or rules and regulations that can be implicit or explicit and that will function as a compliance framework not only in day-to-day matters, but, in particular, in specific cases of conflict.

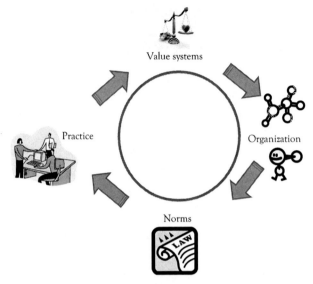

Value systems

Practice

Organization

Norms

Figure 1.2. Circular pattern of cultural development.

Finally, there is practice, or the application of the norms, which reinforces them through public example of what can be considered as "good" or "bad" (Figure 1.2).

The entire system, in fact, acts as a frequent reminder of the values that hold the subculture together, making cultures and subcultures perennial due to the cyclical reinforcement patterns through which they develop.

In other words, cultures tend to remain stable. But having said that, culture change *does* occur when a specific, major event takes place, resulting in the alteration of an otherwise relatively stable equilibrium. If something "big" and "unexpected" happens, the system will have to respond by changing the dynamics of the patterns.

Significant cultural change takes place in general when there is an important mutation in the environment that requires restructuring or reorganization of the social arrangements. A significant technological development, a revolutionary scientific discovery, a war, colonization, and a big pandemic are examples of changes in the environment that could cause cultural change because they could challenge the previously established mental programming and force people to think differently.

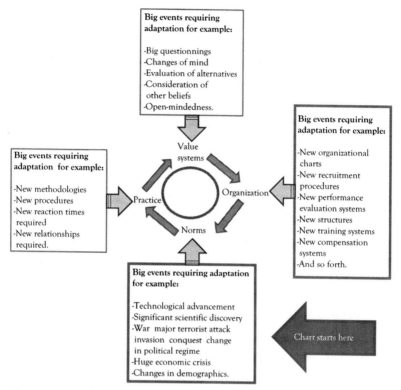

Big events requiring adaptation for example:

-Big questionnings
-Changes of mind
-Evaluation of alternatives
-Consideration of other beliefs
-Open-mindedness.

Value systems

Big events requiring adaptation for example:

-New organizational charts
-New recruitment procedures
-New performance evaluation systems
-New structures
-New training systems
-New compensation systems
-And so forth.

Big events requiring adaptation for example:

-New methodologies
-New procedures
-New reaction times required
-New relationships required.

Practice   Organization

Norms

Big events requiring adaptation for example:

-Technological advancement
-Significant scientific discovery
-War major terrorist attack invasion conquest change in political regime
-Huge economic crisis
-Changes in demographics.

Chart starts here

Figure 1.3. Culture and subculture stability and change.

Examples of events that have changed cultures and patterns promoting cultural stability are countless (Figure 1.3). Let us mention just some of them.

Examples

1. September 11, 2001: Most Americans discover that they may not be liked worldwide and the feeling of insecurity spreads across the country. More and more citizens vote for Republicans, people think in terms of terrorism, and laws are modified in order to respond to the generalized sense of fear.

2. Henry Ford applies chain manufacturing to the car industry: having a car becomes less exclusive and people start moving more and faster. The GDP of industrialized countries grows exponentially, roads are

created and others improved. The first step into distribution through big commercial chains starts to develop.

3. The contraceptive pill becomes popular in Western societies by 1960: women discover their sexual activity is not necessarily linked to maternity any longer and they revisit their social role claiming independence from men and initiate a revolt that promoted laws such as the right to abortion and workplace equality.

4. Turkey may soon enter the EU: The eternal search for "the common denominator" across all EU countries has been on since its early start. One of the attempts to generate the idea that there was a common past and a sense of unity across member states has been Christianity. The entrance of Turkey into the EU may challenge that belief and underline the need for further definitions. It might perhaps at some stage allow the entrance of Israel to the area, on the same grounds.

Cultural programming is difficult to change because all institutions (government, education, law systems, family structure, religion, habitat, etc.) are founded on values that sustain them. If cultural change is to be produced, then all these structures need to change.

Much energy is required to produce cultural change and not only brilliant ideologists, who find alternative ways of thinking, but also strong champions, ready to move actions forward, are required to produce social change.

Using This Information

This introductory chapter should help executives realize that their views might be subjective, even if most people in their culture agree with them.

There are certainties to which we stick, because we need guidelines for action in life, but these certainties may well be the extreme opposite in other parts of the world.

It can certainly be irritating having to coexist, operate, and even attempt to be profitable when dealing across borders; the exercise may well be exhausting, but it is worth the effort because when one executive understands another, it is easier to anticipate his or her behavior, make plans together, produce synergies, and build new opportunities as a team.

Exercises

1. List the principal values that constitute the mental programming of your own culture.

    _____
    _____
    _____
    _____
    _____
    _____

2. Reflect on some problems that could exist between two persons A and B, who have the following sets of values (hierarchically ordered) and who need to cooperate on a particular project.

A	B
1. Family	1. Fun
2. Religion	2. Money
3. Work	3. Friendship

    How could these two people learn from each other in order to produce more synergy?

    _____
    _____
    _____
    _____
    _____
    _____

3. Imagine a situation in which a conflict of values could be observed in the industry of your choice. How could you intervene to solve it as a manager?

    _____
    _____
    _____
    _____
    _____
    _____

PART II

Frameworks for Cultural Analysis

CHAPTER 2

Frameworks for Cultural Analysis

The Cultural Dimensions of Geert Hofstede

The Aim of This Chapter

This chapter aims at describing the basic and most widely used frameworks for cross-cultural analysis according to Geert Hofstede, who defined what he calls "dimensions" or general aspects in which cultures may be grouped according to commonalities in their mental programming.

Cultures in which gender roles are greatly differentiated and emphasized are known as "masculine" cultures—as opposed to "feminine" ones. Groups in which the collective interests overcome individual ones are called "collectivist" as opposed to "individualist." Mental programmings in which hierarchy is a requirement for social order received the name of "high power distant," and that in which a standard pattern of behaviors is preferred to innovative ones are called "high uncertainty avoidant." Later in his career, Hofstede included the category of long-term versus short-term orientation to differentiate groups in which the emphasis is on saving before spending and those that think that debt encourages hard work.

Hofstede[1] and those who followed his work ranked countries according to how they fitted into these categories and most of their research has evolved into more quantitative ranking of the same sort. In this chapter we will pay less attention to rankings and develop on the meaning, origins, and consequences of each stereotypical mental programming.

Frameworks for Cross-Cultural Analysis

Having discussed the origins of culture, its development, and its tendency to reinvent itself through the years in order to survive, we will proceed to the study of different areas in which cultures may differ. Several authors have intended to categorize cultures according to the collective mental programmings that each society promotes.

Some of the authors who have worked on the subject have collected their data through surveys, others have done so through material obtained during cross-cultural seminars with executives, some have business backgrounds, others are anthropologists, but they have all defined distinctive dichotomic areas in which they could rank cultures according to specific parameters. In this chapter and in the next two we will present the most famous work produced in this sense, and this will be the basis of analysis on which the rest of the book is built.

As previously mentioned, Geert Hofstede is a Dutch business anthropologist whose work in the area of culture and management is known around the world. During the 1960s and 1970s, he conducted surveys of IBM employees in more than 40 countries, asking them questions about their jobs and work settings. Based on these surveys, he identified systematic differences among countries.

He identified four basic dimensions of culture, which he called *individualism/collectivism, power distance, uncertainty avoidance,* and *masculinity/femininity.* In this chapter we will examine each of these dimensions, exploring their origin and developing on their potential consequences for cross-cultural management.

Based on the analysis of his dataset, Hofstede calculated a score for 40 different countries on each of the above-mentioned dimensions. These scores, he stressed, have no absolute value, but are useful only as a way to compare countries.

Individualism/Collectivism (IDV)

The first dichotomic area for study defined by Hofstede is individualism/collectivism.

Individualism describes the tendency of people to see themselves as individuals rather than as members of a group. In individualistic cultures, members are usually concerned with personal achievement, with individual rights, and with independence. In collectivistic cultures, people tend to see themselves first and foremost as part of a group, and may be more concerned about the welfare of the group than about individual welfare. They may value harmony and equality above personal achievement, and may be more concerned about an obligation and duty to other members of the group than about individual rights.

In collectivist societies, people are born to enlarge a family and reinforce a clan that will protect them for as long as they are faithful to it. Loyalty to the family is a key aspect of social recognition, as status will most certainly be linked to it. Each individual is part of a family, and safety and security are strongly dependent on each individual's capacity to remain an appreciated member of the clan. This means that in collective societies "we" is more important than "I," because a person alone will not succeed. Belonging to networks is the key success factor in life and family is considered as the primary and most important one of these networks.

In individualistic societies, on the other hand, each person is meant to take care of himself and of his immediate family. Individuals are brought up "not to need" anyone, as well as taught that "I" is more important than "we" because the main aspect of the mental programming is that one should not bother others or impose himself on others. A strong person should not be a charge on society or other people. Independence is valued. Actually, strength is based on personal initiatives and achievements, whereas in collective societies it is based on acceptance into groups.

Identity is therefore based on each person's achievements and characteristics, rather than on the networks to which this person belongs. In collective societies, in contrast, identity is based on the social groups in which one is included. The school one has attended, the clubs, the family, the area or city in which each one was born, and so forth, place each person within the tacit social ranking the collectivistic culture has defined. Therefore, loyalty to these groups is paramount, as being excluded from them means becoming a pariah with no chance of success in life.

Attachment to companies and organizations is also experienced differently in collective and in individualistic societies. In the former, attachment to the workplace is moral more than legal. This means that the respect that the owner or boss obtains goes beyond the contractual agreement: very often the psychological contract exceeds in importance the value of the clauses that have been signed, and both employer and employee respect each other from their position out of a nonexplicit vow of loyalty and protection. In individualistic societies, attachment to work is more economic than ethical or affective, and therefore changes in jobs are more frequent and less traumatic. Market rules tend to influence behavior in companies more often than not.

The fact that in collectivist societies groups provide individuals with security and opportunities also allows them to intervene in the private lives of people. This means that the group will usually indicate what convictions the individual should defend, the friends of the individual should be approved by the group, and the individual is constantly reminded of the obligations he has vis-à-vis the group. Individual ideology must be coherent with group ideology. In individualistic societies, the opposite occurs: autonomy, truth, pleasure, and financial security are enhanced and supported by these cultures, not only as an indicator of success and good social behavior, but also and very specifically as a strong collective need for common growth.

Friendships in collectivistic societies are stable and long-term and also a reflection of the status of a person. People of higher classes or castes are not expected to mix with those of lower backgrounds because that would damage their image and therefore their capacity to remain within privileged circles. In individualistic societies, having diverse friends is possible and these do not necessarily have to mix as the private life of each person is expected to have different and diverse areas that do not necessarily interact (i.e., one person can have friends from a tennis club who are very wealthy, but also friends from camping who are not so wealthy, and still live two sorts of private lives with these groups never having to mingle).

The rankings produced by Hofstede can now be considered out of date, although his followers and disciples keep updating them through research that can be easily found in websites. Nevertheless, the concepts derived from the research are still valid.

As for the origins of individualism, those are arguable, but some hypotheses have been put forward to explain potential factors that could influence the development of this kind of thinking in a defined population.

Wealth could in some cases be the cause of individualism, as nations in which each person is wealthy enough not to depend on others could explain a mental programming in which people do not feel the need to justify their actions to the community. Wealth in some cases could also be the consequence of individualism, as the wealthier one becomes, the more independence is claimed.

Evidently, it would make no sense to say that all wealthy nations are individualistic and all poor ones are collectivistic, as there are examples that would quite clearly contradict these assumptions. In any case, mental programmings are not the result of the influence of one dimension alone, but the conjunction of an indefinite number of factors. Having said this, each dimension defined by Hofstede has been recognized as strongly affecting national culture's mental programming.

For instance, there are many examples of rich nations that score high on collectivism: Japan and Singapore, just to name a few. Factors having potentially influenced the upkeep of a collectivistic mind in spite of economic development could be either historical (the social understanding that Japan could have never reconstructed itself after the Second World War had it not been for the serious loyalty and commitment shown by its inhabitants towards their peers), or philosophical (the Confucian principles which make the common good a priority over the individual good).

Religion certainly does affect the level of collectivism within a society. While Roman Catholicism conveys values that reinforce the image of the individual as dependent on the community, and does not necessarily celebrate the creation of wealth as a path to salvation, some Protestant sects like Calvinists conceive hard work, savings accumulation, and the possession of valuable goods without fiercely displaying them not only as the result of hard work itself (work being perceived as the activity that keeps man out of mischief), but also as a divine blessing. In Roman Catholic communities the rich are expected to give back to the poor (or to the Church), either in kind or in actions (or both). In Protestant communities, sharing is interpreted as a social cohesion activity, but yet everyone should be held responsible for their own actions and the development of their own wealth through work and effort.

Another potential explanation for the development of individualism is linked to industrialization. In view of the type of work required in agricultural societies, teamwork and loyalty to the family or close connections are meant to be beneficial for the deployment of tasks and actions. People work for those they know from very early in their lives, and codependence is necessary for survival. In industrialized societies, on the other hand, each person works for himself, by himself, and far from home (in cities) and for a stranger (a boss). Wherever social mobility is possible, it happens individually and not collectively through promotions. Therefore, countries that industrialized early in history tend to be more individualistic than those having had to rely on agriculture for longer. We will discuss matters relating to the new postindustrialized culture in subsequent chapters.

Power Distance (PDI)

Power distance captures the degree to which members accept an uneven distribution of power. In high power distance cultures, a wide gap is perceived to exist among people at different levels of the hierarchy. Subordinates accept their inferior positions, and are careful to show proper respect and deference to their bosses. Managers, in turn, may issue directives rather than seek broad participation in decision making. In low power distance countries, managers may be less concerned with status and more inclined to allow participation, and their employees may be less deferential and more willing to speak out.

Hofstede has demonstrated that the dimensions operate in similar ways at different levels of analysis, meaning not only that in a power distant society employees and their employers will act as described above, but also that all other structures work in a similar manner as well. Families in high power distant societies are generally led by fathers who control very strongly, and governments are more autocratic in their actions (even in democracies). In fact, high power distance societies are more prone to accept dictatorships than low power distance ones, because the image of a highly powerful presence has been built into the mental programming of their people from an early age (at family level, then through the school structure, then at work, etc.).

Origins of high power distance are uncertain, and so is the origin of most of the frameworks for cultural analysis, but a few hypotheses can be put forward to at least attempt to explain this behavior.

One of the hypotheses is that in benign, warm climates, access to food and basic goods was traditionally simple. No matter how harsh the situation, there has always been a way to survive without the need for strict discipline, planning, and sacrifice. Therefore, the use of structured forces and a firm discipline coming from someone else would be understood as a desirable factor that would motivate towards a collectively organized productive effort. In cold, difficult weathers, nevertheless, the necessary self-discipline "to put work before play" was paramount for each individual in order to survive. For instance, if someone in Finland decided that he would rather sleep than search for food one day, his survival would not be ensured for the next day: discipline had to come from within. This hypothesis explains therefore why generally (and there are many exceptions to this very general rule) in warmer climates people are more inclined to accept power distance than in colder ones. In colder climates, everyone trusts discipline and self-restraint, and therefore social order need not be imposed from the outside, whereas in warmer climates traditionally there has been a need to have someone instill it in spite of the will of others. In general, in high power distance countries wealth is concentrated within the higher stratas of society, whereas in low power distance countries it is more distributed. Money being very closely related to power, this commonality is not very surprising.

Another possible explanation for the origins of power distance is the size of countries. Smaller countries have allowed for plural participation very early in their development simply because it is easier to manage smaller groups of people than large ones. Extensive lands with diverse populations (i.e., Russia) call for centralized lines of command and generalist rules to be applied across the territory. Smaller structures can be run with the participation of many, as their size is still manageable.

We had mentioned some generalities that could sometimes explain the origins of power distance; nevertheless, it is worthwhile signaling that there are many exceptions to these rules. For instance, France and Belgium are both wealthy countries with relatively cold weather, but they still are high power distant. The causes for this exception to the very general rule can include historical facts such as the origin of the two countries in question as part of the Roman Empire. In fact, whereas Germanic societies were run by councils of citizens assembled to make decisions, all Romans would report to an Emperor who had full power. Another difference between the two ancient societies was that in the Latin world, heritage was divided between all brothers once the father of a family died, which implied that a son of a wealthy family would remain a landlord from birth to death. In contrast, in Germanic societies, it was the eldest son who inherited everything, leaving all younger siblings on their own, having to find their own ways to survive and therefore going overnight from belonging to a high society to having nothing to live upon. Social mobility has been a common feature within Germanic societies for a long time, whereas such has not been the case within the Roman Empire.

People in high positions from high power distance cultures in general use and promote the use of status symbols: bosses would not eat lunch at the same cafeteria as their employees, they would have private lifts, private parking slots, inaccessible diaries... Areas of the city would be very much divided according to social rank and power structures.

In high power distance cultures, authorities are either charismatic or constraining. Their power is not the result of authority and competence, but just the result of political games based on delusional demagogy, traditional access to hierarchy, or imposition by force. The person in charge is not necessarily the one that "can do the best job," but the one that can have the masses follow him/her (more frequently him than her). Wage structures show significant differences in high power distance companies, whereas they do not in low power distance ones, in which everyone accesses the same level of education and where higher education is not always necessary to access power.

These reasons make it very clear why stable democracies are most frequently found in low power distance cultures, where it is not made obvious to everyone early on in their lives that there are undisputable ranks in life that ought not to be challenged. Statistics have shown that in high power distance cultures the ideological breach between labor and conservatives is highly polarized, whereas in low power distance cultures, the search for consensus between extremes is seen as a means to minimize exhausting and costly conflicts. Unions, for instance, are generally organized by companies or by governments in high power distance cultures, whereas they are less ideological and more practical in low power distance ones, in which their actions, by the way, are visible in day-to-day results.

There is certainly a link between religion and power distance. The Roman Catholic Church is visibly hierarchical in structure (with many ranks within the clerical order), and its philosophy is based on dogmas and absolute truths (i.e. the virginity of Holy Mary, the existence of a Holy Trinity, etc.). The Pope is formally considered as a full-power decision maker and rules apply worldwide. The Protestant tradition, on the other hand, is decentralized, has very little structure, and rules are adapted to local practitioners. Hence, Roman Catholic countries show in most cases high power distance as Protestant ones are more low power distant. In the case of the Muslims, even if their Church structure is not hierarchical in shape, their philosophy strongly supports high power distance behaviors, as stated in many passages of the Koran (i.e., "Men like to obey" or "Those who obey the Prophets obey God").

Uncertainty Avoidance (UAI)

Uncertainty avoidance describes the extent to which people seek to avoid, or feel threatened by ambiguous or risky situations. Individuals in cultures characterized by high uncertainty avoidance may be risk averse in trying new ways of doing things, in starting new companies, in changing jobs, or in welcoming outsiders. They may emphasize continuity and stability rather than innovation and change. In cultures of low uncertainty avoidance, members may more readily embrace change, may show more initiative, and may be more accepting of different views and new ideas.

In low uncertainty avoidance cultures rules are ambiguous, unconventional behaviors are tolerated and there is solidarity towards those who do not belong to the mainstream. In high uncertainty avoidance cultures, there is a stronger need for rules, and there is stability, in particular in the work environment.

Latin countries are in general high uncertainty controllers, whereas Anglo-Saxons, Northern Europeans, South East Asians, Africans, and Indians show lower scores in this sense.

The roots of uncertainty avoidance could be found in the origins of Latin countries, namely in the Roman Empire and its unique legislative system that applied in all territories and across all the cultures in order to control them. Centralized rule derived from constitutional law, which is unique, undisputable, and supposed to reflect the general values that ought to be applied to as many cases as foreseeable. On the opposite extreme, there is the Anglo system of Common Law, which relies on juris-prudence, rather than on the rational formulas that would need to be applied to all situations everywhere.

A unique system with a generic law that develops into branches guar-antees anxiety management, as there is always a formal support to the decisions being made. Strict rules provide with certainty as one knows what is good and what is bad and what the consequences of deviant behavior will be. Low uncertainty avoidance cultures conceive truths applicable "on the spot" that may not apply to other cases.

As far as religion is concerned, high uncertainty avoidance cultures stick to dogmas and absolute truths, whereas popular religions in low uncertainty avoidance cultures insist on initiative, self-guidance, and are more accepting of the evolution of the notion of morality across time and therefore their rules are modified rather more frequently than not. Roman Catholicism scores high in uncertainty avoidance, intermediary results are shown by Judaism and Islam, whereas Protestantism, Bud-dhism, and Animism are considered low uncertainty avoidance religions in view of their normative structure, which is less inflexible.

The same reasoning applies to knowledge. In fact, great scientists from high uncertainty avoidance cultures have based their theories on absolute truths and their mode of thinking is more deductive (they search for an undeniable fact and then derive all truth from it), rather than inductive (deriving truth from a common factor found in many cases). Examples of this difference are numerous: Kant's Critique of Pure Reason (attempting to find the absolute rightful and all-applicable norms for ethical behavior no matter the circumstances), Marx, Weber, Descartes, etc.

The case study method as a research method and a pedagogic tool was created in Anglo-Saxon countries and that is where it has progressed. The same theories are perceived with discomfort in high uncertainty avoid-ance cultures, as they are based on specific, particular events rather than on generic, irrefutable ideas.

Delegation in companies is more likely to occur in low uncertainty avoidance cultures, as risks are perceived as part of the game. In high uncertainty avoidance cultures, delegating could be assumed to be a risky choice, in particular if power is given to people who are younger, of lower social rank, or diverse. The preference for "what has worked in the past" will be made in most cases. Foreigners, for instance, are more likely to have their chance of becoming managers in low uncertainty avoidance cultures than in high uncertainty avoidance ones, where they will be mistrusted in their capacity to perform their duties. Ambition is also considered as a desirable quality in low uncertainty avoidance cultures, which is not the case in high uncertainty avoidance ones. Technical ability is preferred to managerial skills in high uncertainty avoidance cultures, as the former can be measured and tested, whereas the latter are more subjective.

Failure is frightening in high uncertainty avoidance societies, and is seriously punished whereas it can be considered as necessary to evolve in low uncertainty avoidance ones. Working for big companies is preferred in high uncertainty avoidance cultures, and being an entrepreneur is frequently likely to be perceived as a last resort for someone avoiding unemployment.

Masculinity/Femininity (MAS)

Hofstede used the term "masculinity" to represent a cultural preference for achievement, assertiveness, and material success, and "femininity" to describe a greater importance placed on maintaining relationships, on caring for members, and on a high quality of life. In so-called masculine countries, work-related values tend to favor achievement and competition. In so-called feminine countries, firms provide more extensive services for the well-being of members, and emphasize overall welfare rather than bottom-line performance.

It is commonly believed within academic circles that the main origin of this difference lies in the way boys and girls are socialized since early childhood. Indeed, in societies in which male and female roles are very much differentiated, the general paradigm becomes masculine and in cultures in which girls and boys are brought up in similar ways, the feminine mental programming prevails.

For instance, in feminine societies, girls will have both mother and father as role models and so will boys. Both girls and boys will be responsible for helping set up the table and do the dishes, both boys and girls will learn to clean their rooms and boys and girls will be objects of the same professional expectations from their parents regarding their future career prospects. In masculine societies, expectations differ from an early age: girls are expected to learn how to run a household and take care of their families, whereas boys are brought up to be strong and powerful, have important careers, and earn money.

The result of such a differentiated education is that in feminine societies both men and women are expected to show their feelings to the same extent, both men and women have career aspirations, both men and women share household duties, and both men and women can access power positions in society. This is all much more relative in masculine societies.

As far as values are concerned, in masculine societies both men and women appreciate what are commonly referred to as masculine values: having a car with a huge powerful engine could be extremely appealing to men, and men possessing such an item would certainly seem appealing to girls. In feminine societies, having a car that is respectful of the environment could be important for both men and women.

The origins of femininity in cultures are uncertain, but it is quite common to find feminine societies in colder areas of the planet. Historically, in such latitudes, only one person being in charge of looking for food was not enough, that is why it is supposed that both women and men have been expected to assume responsibilities in "bringing home the bacon" for centuries. Equality in roles is in general more necessary when chances of survival in rough conditions need to be maximized as well as the size of the working population. Dissimilarity in gender roles is more frequent in warm countries because survival and growth of the population usually depended less on the action of humans on nature. In such a situation, women could afford to remain aside from certain practices because less manpower was necessary to survive.

In the specific case of ancient Scandinavia, Viking women have had to assume political positions while their husbands were abroad, which explains to some extent the historical evolution in countries such as Sweden or Norway, in which feminine values prevail.

In feminine countries, it is considered very important that everyone has what is necessary to live in dignified ways. Basic schooling, right to a home, and health are priorities for everyone. In masculine societies there is less solidarity and everyone is concerned for their families, relatives, or relations much more than for the common good. For similar reasons, feminine cultures are more prone to support ventures that protect the environment and to donate money to charities or international development activities.

With regard to the influence of religion on masculinity, it is possible to establish a link between the history of Judeo-Christianity and a historical evolution from masculinity towards femininity in religious paradigms. Indeed, in the Old Testament God appears as a powerful creature often referred to as a Judge that punishes and imposes a supranatural law, there are very few female characters, and the rules are very strict and well defined by the prophets. In Catholicism, there are already a few more feminine beliefs; Jesus is poor, modest, lives surrounded by fishermen and prostitutes, promoting love and forgiveness. The character of a woman, the Mother, Holy Mary brings an aspect of tenderness to his actions. In Protestantism, femininity is pushed one step further: the Mother is not a virgin any more, women can be ordained pastors and ministers, the notion of hell is less prominent, and communitarian work based on solidarity is extensively promoted. Divorce is allowed within the Church.

As for the influence of masculinity/femininity at work, in feminine countries both young men and young women take up challenging careers, whereas it is mainly men who do that in masculine cultures. In masculine countries it is more unusual to find women in higher positions, but the few that get there exhibit very aggressive behavior, as if this was the only way to compete with their male counterparts. There is less tension at work in feminine cultures and fewer industrial conflicts.

Long-term/Short-term Orientation (LTO)

With the increasing power of East Asian economies during the early 1980s, however, Hofstede wondered if his four indices had adequately captured what he perceived as the distinctive cultural characteristics of East Asian cultures: diligence, patience, and frugality. Based on further research, Hofstede added a fifth dimension that he referred to as long-term orientation.

Long-term orientation societies focus on the future, which means that they follow cultural trends towards delaying immediate gratification; therefore, they are money-saving societies. Short-term orientation societies focus on the past and on the present, respecting traditions and following trends in spending even if this means borrowing money.

Origins for this last dimension are not specified, but philosophical ideas found in Confucianism are compatible with the behavior shown by many Asian societies in this respect. Spending only once savings have been made is considered a sign of wisdom. In more action-oriented societies, spending on the spot to pay later can be understood as a motivator for action. It is sometimes to pay off debts that people take on overtime or make efforts to pay for what they have bought in the past.

Amongst regions scoring high in long-term orientation are China, Hong Kong, Taiwan, Japan, and South Korea. Top short-term oriented countries are Pakistan, the Philippines, and Bangladesh. Western countries also are considered as short-term oriented.

Synthesis

Geert Hofstede, a business anthropologist, questioned himself about ways in which people from different cultures were different. Then, he took up a huge study, which consisted of interviewing employees of IBM all over the world.

Hofstede observed four different dimensions and categorized cultures with regard to their:

- Hierarchical distance,
- Reactions towards uncertainty,
- Individualism level,
- Masculinity level.
- And much later on relationship to the future (long-term versus short-term orientation)

Characteristics of his classification are detailed below.

Individualism Versus Collectivism

Characteristic	Individualism	Collectivism
Ways of spending time	Alone	With other people
Level of technical development	High	Low
Dependence on companies	Low (economic)	High (moral)
Families	Nuclear	Huge
Wealth	Rich	Not that rich
Religion	Protestantism	Many others
Industrialization	Modern	Traditional
Social mobility	High	Low
Weather	Cold	Warm
Politics	Democracy	Dictatorships

Masculinity Versus Femininity

Characteristic	Masculinity	Femininity
Roles	Defined	Ambiguous
Climate	Warm	Cold
Relation to ecology	Not sensitive	Sensitive
Career choice	Different for women and men	Similar for women and men
Religion	Traditional	New
Climate at work	Tense	Relaxed

Hierarchical Distance

Characteristic	High Power Distance	Short Power Distance
Climate	Mediterranean (warm)	Cold
Size of countries	Big	Small
Distribution of wealth	Concentrated	Distributed
Attitudes	Show difference	Dissimulate difference

(Continued)

(*Continued*)

Characteristic	High Power Distance	Short Power Distance
Religions	Hierarchical (ex. Roman Catholics)	Without formal hierarchy (ex. Protestants)
Ideology	Conflict (Machiavelli)	Consensus
Politics	Dictatorships	Democracy
Companies	Bureaucracies	More fluent communications between different levels

Uncertainty Avoidance

Characteristic	High Control	Low Control
Type of countries	Latin	Others
Laws	Specific	Open
Attitude	Conservatives	Initiatives, risks
Religion	Life after death Absolute truth Hierarchical	Buddhism Hinduism Animism
Science	Pure truth	Pragmatism

Using This Information

Managers aware of how their international counterparts think, feel, and react according to their mental programming can obtain significant competitive advantage over those who just act in front of others as they would at home and expect them to behave the same way they do.

It is nevertheless important to clarify that stereotyping is never good, and a culturally sensitive international manager who has been trying to act as he or she interprets one normally behaves in your country might find it offensive that you just try to classify or stamp on each one of his or her behaviors (i.e., saying out loud in an attempt to look open-minded, "Oh, you have to phone your parents in the middle of the day because you are collectivist"—it could well happen that the business person had to phone home in the middle of the day because his or her father had to undergo heart surgery that morning and he/she needs to know whether everything went well).

In most cases, when studying Hofstede's frameworks, executives worldwide just think "Oh, that is why they act so weird! Knowing that, I shall change my attitude/adapt it so that we can deal with each other better." It helps very much to understand where the other party is coming from and the frameworks allow us to formulate hypotheses that should allow us to tolerate, understand, and find avenues for conflict avoidance and resolution; rather than to stereotype and blame those who challenge our behavioral expectations.

Questions

1. Where would you place the following countries along each of Hofstede's cultural dimensions? Give examples.

USA

_____

_____

_____

_____

China

_____

_____

_____

_____

France

_____

_____

_____

_____

Germany

_____

_____

_____

_____

Japan

_____
_____
_____
_____

Russia

_____
_____
_____
_____

2. Now go to http://www.geert-hofstede.com/ and find out how
    Hofstede classified each country. Do you agree with his scoring?
    Why/why not? Explain your answer.

_____
_____
_____
_____

CHAPTER 3

Frameworks for Cultural Analysis According to Fons Trompenaars

Contextualizing Background Information

Fons Trompenaars and Charles Hampden-Turner[1] have produced frameworks for cultural analysis based on their observations of behavior in companies and also through the collection of data from executive workshops. Even if their methodology has been widely contested by authors from traditional research backgrounds such as Geert Hofstede, who think Trompenaars' methodology is not rigorous enough, their models have been widely used both in business and in academia for the last few decades.

Some of the frameworks designed by business consultants Trompenaars and Hampden-Turner overlap with those of Hofstede, in particular individualism versus collectivism. Other frameworks are either different or point at the same parameter from a different angle.

Locus of Control

This framework, based on Julian Rotter's[2] categories, defines our relationship with our environment. On one extreme, we have "External Locus of Control" cultures, in which people understand humans as part of nature and therefore must go along with its laws, directions, and forces. On the other extreme, "Internal Locus of Control" cultures are described as those in which people feel they need to master the universe and everything in it in order not to be dominated by its forces. In their minds there is always a dominant and a surrendered, so when deciding whether to adapt to a situation or not it is best to choose not to, as adapting is normally interpreted as a defeat.

The "control" of the world can be interpreted in different ways. Through study and creation we can understand nature and therefore master it through the construction of bridges, dams, and better ways of living. Credit is strictly and specifically allocated to those contributing to innovation and to the discovery of more effective tools that could help the community to live better. A person stealing credit from someone else would be condemned for plagiarism, which is generally considered as a very serious offence by internal locus of control cultures as the search for superior forms of quality life is to be strongly encouraged.

"Control" can also be interpreted as the imposition of one's own practices over someone else's. Therefore, in an international merger between companies from internal locus of control cultures, if one party imposes operational procedures, the other will naturally tend to reject them without even giving them much consideration, as this attitude would be interpreted as an attempt to control them.

On the other hand, when dealing with external locus of control cultures, the same company would not face rejection of the procedures, which would even be gratefully received by the other company as new resources to enrich their lives. In fact, they might copy them and resell them, as ideas are not considered as concrete elements belonging to anyone, but simply an element of the environment that surrounds them and is being made available for their use.

The Disneyland Paris case is an excellent example of how similarity in cultural perceptions can often lead to conflict, rather than facilitating interactions. Indeed, when Disney set up in external locus of control Japan, the local society welcomed the company and was delighted to incorporate elements brought in by American procedures and common uses in their own culture after having adapted them. They combined Mickey Mouse and Hello Kitty in a very clever manner, teenagers started considering visits to the attraction park as a traditional step in their dating routine, and overall they "Japanized" Disney rather than perceiving the company as an invader from the West. As an external locus of control culture, they were eager to absorb anything new from the West.

On the other hand, when Disney arrived in internal locus of control France, the society rejected their presence not only because of the perceived image of America as an "Empire," but also because their practices were considered as a threat to the French way of living and to French values. The "no alcohol in premises" rule was interpreted as "your French wine is not welcome here"; the hire and fire policy was heard as "your French employment laws are not welcome here"; the dress codes were interpreted as "your French fashion is not welcome here"; etc. Overall, Disney in France was interpreted by the French as a serious attempt to control and master French culture by the Americans. It took many years for Disney to revisit their communication strategy and alter their image in France.

Examples of Common Thoughts or Perceptions Typical of Internal/External Locus of Control Cultures

Situation	Internal Locus of Control	External Locus of Control
An Asian company copies a fashion design and produces it massively and at a lower price.	"They steal our products. We need to react by promoting copyright laws and reinforcing them."	"We can certainly take these designs, slightly alter them to fit our markets, sell cheaper and make everybody profit from this initiative."
Someone has a headache	"Painkillers will deal with it."	"We need to find natural elements in the environment that will enrich us with their healing powers by reinforcing our natural systems and/or we need to practice activities that keep us in close contact with nature." (tai-chi, acupuncture, yoga, etc.)
With regards to integrating into a new culture	"We are just what we are and who we are, we keep our ways wherever we go." "In France we all eat pork at the school cafeteria and nobody is allowed to wear veils."	"We absorb new ways and mix them to what is typically ours, producing a mix that contains *the best of both worlds*."

(Continued)

Situation	Internal Locus of Control	External Locus of Control
When dealing with foreign partners	"We need to impose our rules and control as much as we can. Everyone likes our products and our way of operating." or "Never trust foreigners, we deal with them if under pressure, but in the end when the moment of truth comes, they will always choose to protect themselves."	"Let's see what they have to bring to us. Their technologies are probably powerful and interesting, how could we make the most of them and blend them with our own ways and items?"
In science	"We make a hypothesis and deduce, the principle is correct only if the predicted result follows." "We need to understand in order to control and predict and then control again."	"We analyze what is available to us from nature or from other sources. We interpret it, complete it, and enhance our understanding of the world with the new information we could gather."
When testing/trying a foreign product	"Are they testing our patriotism? Why do we want this foreign thing?"	"Oh, it's new, it's interesting, it is appealing."
In managerial techniques	"We design business strategies, business objectives, we measure them, we control performance based on them."	"We cannot control the world around us, we need to adapt. Adaptation makes us stronger, there is little prediction involved in our lives."
With regards to the boss	"We negotiate, we look for arrangements, we develop power struggles, or we surrender."	"The boss is there to guide us and protect us. If we are loyal, we will not lack the necessities."

(Continued)

(*Continued*)

Situation	Internal Locus of Control	External Locus of Control
With regards to pay for performance	"Performance is determined if not solely at least mainly by each individual's capacity and will to perform."	"Performance does not only depend on the individual being evaluated. There are external aspects that will have an influence and that are alien to the individual's will and capacity to perform. Also, we have to take into consideration other aspects such as the manager's relationship to the individual to be evaluated, the position of the individual in the company, relationships with external stakeholders, etc."
When making decisions or signing contracts	"We are as specific and as detailed as we can be in order to avoid trouble later. If possible, we have lawyers involved."	"We cannot control what happens around us, therefore it does not make much sense to attempt to cover all possible scenarios. We prefer to write ambiguous contracts and to trust our relationship to be able to solve any particular problems that may arise on the way. Lawyers cannot help much as they are also unable to master the forces that determine performance, they just warn us about the fact that the potential partner might be anticipating conflict."

Sequentials and Synchronics

Fons Trompenaars and Charles Hampden-Turner have defined as "sequentials," cultures in which people imagine time as a succession of passing events that never repeat themselves. In this sense, the past, present, and future are not tightly interrelated or interconnected. What happened in the past is to be forgotten, the present is to be lived, and the future is to be planned. There are also other cultures (synchronic) in which the past, the present, and the future are tightly linked and cannot be separated. The present is at least partially the result of what happened in the past, and the future will be affected by our actions. A mistake may not be very easily forgotten or forgiven because its consequences will not just affect the present, but also the future. Performance in synchronic cultures will be tied to several factors that go beyond "the last man's act," which may not be the case with the sequentials.

In synchronic cultures, long-term relationships are of key relevance, because those that we have helped in the past will feel obliged to help us in the future. If we hurt or offend someone, this will come back to us sooner or later, as time is perceived and conceived as a returning factor. Since mistakes are more easily tolerated in sequential cultures, risk taking is more likely to occur.

Time is considered differently in sequential and in synchronic cultures. In sequential cultures, it is perceived as a valuable, precious, and rare asset. In most cases, it can be measured in monetary terms and it should therefore not be wasted. People show respect by being punctual, as we all are worth the same and arriving late to meetings or gatherings means in a way that time is being "stolen" from the other person, who could have made different arrangements otherwise and therefore used what is his/hers to his/her own benefit. Time is an asset that if managed well can lead to success and personal growth, and not allowing other people to decide how to use it best by arriving late can be seen as a sign of disinterest, lack of compassion, and/or rudeness.

In synchronic cultures, on the other hand, time is interpreted as a means to define and underline each person's role and position in society. The acknowledging of the other person's role is made by "giving time." In synchronic cultures, it is normal to expect senior members to arrive later than junior ones to meetings. This way it is made clear who holds the primary role in society and who "gives time." Seniors are not expected to lead by example in being on time or not interrupting meetings. On the contrary, they need to display their superior status by acting in exactly the opposite manner from their subordinates. Waiting or making others wait is a tool to signal status and power. For instance, in a similar manner, in synchronic cultures, sellers are expected to wait for buyers (buyers have the money); men can wait for women (it is considered as an act of gallantry to wait for a lady in a bar, whereas the other way round is very rude), and younger for older (synchronics often tend to show appreciation towards seniority as it is widely considered that learning takes time). Status, in synchronic cultures is tightly linked to time, respect, and hierarchy.

Also, in synchronic cultures, time is used mainly to develop trust through relationship building. Dinners are important for business, even if only personal topics are discussed during them. In synchronic cultures, you do business with people you know. And getting to know people takes time. Sequentials, who assume that there is time for business and time for socializing can easily feel unsettled by what they consider as a waste of time. Synchronics can be irritated by sequentials' lack of sensitivity and tact when showing disinterest in developing a relationship, which for synchronics is the most effective way to avoid trouble in the future.

The following situations illustrate behavioral differences in synchronic versus sequential cultures.

Situation 1

Jim Crafton, a 29-year-old salesman from a small paper company in Missouri, thought it would be a great idea to visit his Greek business partners on his way back home from his honeymoon in Cyprus. So on the last few days of his trip, he made a few phone calls and made arrangements for a few on-the-spot appointments.

Jim managed to arrive on time for the first two meetings with client companies, unlike the local businessmen, who only showed up 15 to 20 minutes after schedule. So, the day of the third meeting, he decided to take the morning to visit a few historical sites with his wife and arrived

20 minutes late at the company, convinced that he was not being rude, just acting local.

This is a typical case of an executive acting in total disrespect of local customs. Not only did he not acknowledge his relatively lower status (being younger, from the selling side, and belonging to a small company) when visiting his business partners "on his way back from a trip" (this lack of delicacy may have been punished by his partners' tardiness, in an attempt to remind him of WHO is the higher status party), but on top of that, he did not get to his last meeting on time. There is no doubt that his product should be either exceedingly superior in comparison to his competitors' or that his price must be much lower for this deal to close.

Situation 2

Patrick Bengey arrived in Riyadh, in Saudi Arabia, hoping he would be able to depart on the very next day with his contract signed in order to start his holidays with peace of mind the following week.

He was greeted very formally at the airport, and then driven in a limousine to a huge office where he was extremely well received by Dr. Mandallah, a high-ranking government official, and his numerous crew, all present at the meeting.

Patrick was eager to get to the "nitty gritty," start focusing on the business matter exclusively and as soon as possible, but his counterpart had arrived over an hour late (Patrick was kept waiting, even though entertained by numerous servants and just people talking to him about generalities of life in the USA), plus when he arrived, Dr. Mandallah only wanted to exchange pleasantries, and show him around.

At some point, Patrick urged Dr. Mandallah to start the negotiation, but he was told that it was a very sensitive matter that needed to be discussed in private, later on.

Getting down to business in synchronic cultures takes time. This is an indisputable fact. One cannot expect to close a deal in cultures in which "giving time" means "respecting others," by rushing things over or by pushing. The only natural consequence of such behavior will be reticence, distrust, and having the business partner think that one does not really want to do business.

The time spent by Patrick in small talk and in waiting was not time gone to waste. It was time invested in developing a trust relationship between the partners. During this time, the "candidate" to become a business partner was thoroughly studied and analyzed. His product may or may not have been the best, but his capacity to develop and sustain relationships would have been scrutinized in detail.

This type of behavior from the synchronic partner is not illogical at all. In environments where law systems are lengthy and perhaps unreliable, time spent making sure a deal will not end up with conflict of interests becomes a good investment. Because of the time spent in developing trust and mutual support, the chances that one of the parties will switch providers or suppliers or even do anything that could jeopardize the relationship are minimized.

Investing in "getting to know" the potential business partner provides a guarantee that once trust is in place business will flow without unexpected surprises and costly and ineffective lawsuits. Dr. Mandallah will probably pick the businesspartner that offers him a good interpersonal relationship, besides an interesting deal.

Situation 3

Tom, an American businessman, was visiting his supplier in Brazil. He was very excited about the deal and was hoping to have the contract signed within 24 hours in order to make sure production would start with enough buffer time in advance.

Once in Sao Paolo, Tom was invited to join the team for a meal, which lasted for three long hours, during which the origin and making of each dish was explained, wine tasting took place and talks developed from sports to current affairs, family stories, and compliments about the weather.

By teatime, Tom started to get anxious, because when he finally thought they could get into the signing part, his supplier suggested playing a tennis match before dinner.

Tom did not know whether to be delighted, disappointed, or angry, but he did start to suspect that he would not have signed the contract within the next day or two.

There is no doubt that Tom will NOT get his contract signed within the desired 24 hours and he will probably not have it signed within the next week or so either.

The Brazilian friendly approach is a sign of interest in developing a business relationship that will hopefully develop long-term business deals that will multiply in the future as well. An investment in trust and goodwill relationships is therefore paramount to guarantee the successful development of business deals.

By showing his guest around and sharing sports practice on a sunny day, the Brazilian partner is actually "giving time" to his potential counterpart. He is therefore clearly signaling a lively interest in having the relationship develop into fruitful future contracts and joint activities. No cushion time is needed when good relationships are set: friends will always help when necessary to catch up with delays and by absorbing inconveniences.

Tom should relax and enjoy, as this would probably be the best way to make sure the deals are closed and that the partner will not just comply with the agreements they would have jointly developed to everyone's benefit. Paying too much attention to the hurrying from headquarters and being eager to get results could ruin the whole endeavor. Nothing could be more harmful to this very promising business relationship than a misplaced comment suggesting business is more important, or more urgent, or exclusive of the time he is cordially invited to spend with the Brazilian partner. Needless to say (not always needless, actually), any suggestion that Latin cultures are not keen to work and that they spend their time having fun or that they are lazy (which would be a natural interpretation of the behavior by a Saxon) would definitely lead to the end of the matter and probably of any potential deal happening with anyone directly and perhaps even indirectly connected to the supplier.

In this case, the suggestion for Tom is simple: use this week to improve his tennis service and his smash during the following week, as believe it or not this will be the best way to turn your time into sustainable profits (there are good perks attached to doing business with synchronic cultures indeed).

Particularism Versus Universalism

In certain cultures what ensures stability, progress, and growth is mainly respect of norms and obligations that are determined by society and sometimes established by law. Respect of these rules is paramount to the development of peaceful relationships and general harmony. It is generally assumed that breaking such rules could eventually lead to chaos and therefore exceptions should be avoided. In case of trouble, rules, lawyers, and the established formal system will intervene to solve the problems in a systematic way.

In other cultures, on the other hand, it is widely believed that in fact what promotes harmony and security is not rules, but good relationships. Exceptions and the individual examination of each case, with particular attention being given to specific individuals with whom favors can be exchanged, are important. In case of trouble, it is friends or people we have either helped in the past or who could expect us to help them in the future who will intervene to solve problems in a spontaneous way. Give-give situations are therefore unavoidable, as sometimes formalized rules can be wrong, inapplicable, or perhaps in many cases they could have been developed with the personal interests of the powerful and the corrupt in mind rather than the common good. And people have to be there to fix them on a case-by-case basis. These cultures are called "particularistic cultures."

Examples of Common Thoughts or Perceptions Which Appear as Typical of Universal and Particularistic Cultures

Situation	Universalist type of thinking	Particularistic type of thinking
Regarding equality	Exceptions should be avoided, as they weaken rules. Everyone should be equally treated by law regardless of background.	This person is not "a citizen" to me. He/she is my friend/colleague/sister/son, etc. and therefore my duty is to protect him/her no matter what the rules say. It would be unethical **not** to do so.

(Continued)

Situation	Universalist type of thinking	Particularistic type of thinking
Regarding trust	Particularists cannot be trusted because they will always help their friends.	Universalists cannot be trusted because they would betray their friends.
When a friend has been punished for breaking a rule	The law has been broken and if he is not punished, then he will never learn. Look what happens when people break the rules.	Now that my friend is in trouble, he needs more help than ever.
Predominant religion	Protestantism: – Believers relate to God through written laws, – No human intermediaries (i.e. priests in confession) to consider exceptions.	Roman Catholicism: – Relate to God through particular confessions and through a priest, – People can break commandments and still find pity.
The contract	Detailed, with lawyers in negotiations.	Extremely detailed contracts might be interpreted as lack of trust or the only way to ensure accomplishment. There are other reasons than law why people would not cheat. Relationships count more than contracts, which are rather a guideline or an approximation. To keep the relationship at times it is necessary to do more than the contract requires.
Timing for a business trip	Negotiations need to end as soon as possible.	Negotiations aim to develop a sustainable relationship that will last and avoid past trouble. The quality of the product being dealt with is almost as important as the quality of the relationship being established.

(*Continued*)

(*Continued*)

Situation	Universalist type of thinking	Particularistic type of thinking
Role of the Head Office	They have as an aim to direct and assume responsibility for their decisions. They control.	Head office cannot control everything because they are far away and therefore unaware of all particular arrangements, relationships, and situations that determine what happens locally. Sometimes pretending to obey head office is a way to stay on good terms with them, without making mistakes they would make due to their own inexperience and lack of local knowledge.
Job evaluations and rewards	As impersonal as possible, in order to avoid human biases.	Employees seek gratification through relationships to the leader. Being in good terms with the leader is considered as an important asset. The leader decides on promotions not only on the basis of performance, but also considering the quality of the relationship with the employees.

There is a strong link between universalism/particularism and synchronics/sequentials. As developing relationships takes time, and because relationships from the past will last through the present and towards the future, the time invested in relationships inevitably pays off. Exceptions will be made by particularists in order to favor those they trust. Reciprocity is expected.

Particularists often accuse universalists of being corrupt and vice versa. Particularists think it is shameful to treat members of one's family with coldness and in the same way other employees are treated. The same is valid in many cases regarding those who do not share similar backgrounds. It is often interpreted as lack of loyalty ("They do not even help their friends, what sort of people are they?"). In a similar manner, universalists consider particularists as corrupt, because they think every person should be treated in the same way and exceptions should not be tolerated. Universalists often accuse particularists of being unfair ("They always help their friends").

Specifics Versus Diffuses

According to Fons Trompenaars et al., there are cultures in which the status of a person will influence his/her behavior and the perception others have of his behavior in all circumstances. Cultures where this happens more often than in others are called diffuse cultures. In non-diffuse cultures (also called "specific" cultures), status relates to specific situations, when playing specific roles, and is subject to change.

For example, in diffuse cultures as for instance in most of France, the professional role of a senior manager at an important company will spread into all his/her activities, even outside work. In the light of his/her role, such a person should marry someone of similar social status and would not be expected to mix with others from a lower social status (e.g., people would not find it normal that such a person would play tennis with a neighbor who is a factory worker or do his Sunday shopping at the local food market in his sweatpants). In diffuse cultures, one's behavior, way of dressing, and even language will determine the role he plays in society and there is no break from that role. The role will need to be played at all times and in all circumstances.

Even when social differences exist, as they do in most cultures, there are some cultures in which the roles played by each one of us correspond to specific situations and the personal status may vary according to the situations as well. Hence, the way we operate at work may or may not affect our behavior in private. In such cases, it would not be surprising for people to find their senior manager shopping unshaven at the local market on a Sunday morning in his sweatpants or learning that he recently married his maid, who does not come from a privileged background and has no higher education.

Another difference between specific and diffuse cultures is that in the former, and due to the fact that status is restricted to the particular context of each activity, relationships also tend to relate to each activity or status context. In specific cultures, indeed, people usually relate to specific groups in specific manners, having therefore "friends from work," "friends from golf," "friends from the charity," "friends from holidays in Bermuda," etc. Relationships relate to roles and statuses that are specific, do not engulf all actions and are not personality-defining; relationships establish quite quickly and then as quickly vanish, as they only affect restricted areas of a person's life.

People from more specific cultures open up more easily to others and get to know others fast. But these "friendships" or acquaintances can disappear just as quickly. Friends from work, friends from golf, and friends from holidays rarely mix, as the "hat" worn by the person performing these roles is different according to the group they interact with. In diffuse cultures, relationships take longer to be established, but once they have been constructed, loyalty becomes a key value that makes them last longer. Also, relationships affect all areas of the life of a person. Therefore a person will have fewer acquaintances or friends, these relationships may have taken longer to establish, but once the link is developed and strengthened, it affects all areas of the person's life. In this sense, for a typical person from a diffuse culture, there may be "friends met at work," "friends met at golf," etc., but all these friends will probably mix and even belong to the same circles, because they will probably share compatible status and will be looking for external signals to underline this fact.

In specific cultures, for example, friendships and team dynamics can be built during a seminar, an outdoor weekend company activity, or even alongside a conference. Rather immediately, teams could be formed, become operational, and once the objectives that gathered them are accomplished, they would even more quickly dissolve. In diffuse cultures these dynamics sound artificial, as relationships of any kind require time for development. Also, whereas the specific mind can accept the idea of immediately sharing a part of life (professional, relating to the project, specific to a particular activity), the diffuse mind has more difficulties in accepting this fact. In order to relate to someone, to allow someone in your life, it becomes necessary to get to know the person and/or to trust the group. Individuals need to know more about the personal aspects of others before they share time and activities with them. Otherwise, they would not share information or would find working together disturbing.

As individuals from diffuse cultures often circulate within the same circles, whatever goes wrong in their lives will affect their status and relationships in all areas of their life. A mistake, a dismissal, a setback, a failure, or a defeat will be known by his/her whole environment and have consequences in all aspects of his/her life. The notion of "losing face" is therefore typical of diffuse cultures. When succumbing to public shame, individuals from diffuse cultures find refuge nowhere, as everyone will know and there will be no place to which the discomfort will not follow. In specific cultures, on the other hand, the effects of a wrongful situation will hardly expand into all areas of someone's life, as this is somehow compartmentalized and each part of it is restricted to specific people belonging to specific activities and holding different status symbols.

Because people from specific cultures relate to others in specific situations and within limited areas, they can easily engage in the process of developing new acquaintances, as these will be expected to share only a limited number of activities in a restricted area of their lives. The approach of specific people to strangers will therefore be friendlier and without protocol. This may be considered as "cheerful, glamorous, and superficial" by people from diffuse cultures. Inversely, diffuses will require the necessary time and protocol before allowing anyone into their circle, which may lead people from specific cultures to think they are cold, distant, or snobbish.

Achievers Versus Ascribers

The next of Fons Trompenaars' frameworks describes what grants status in different societies. There are some societies in which status comes from what people have actually "achieved" and those in which status is inherited or determined by what people actually "are." These societies are called "ascribed." Status in ascribed societies can originate from age, social class, gender, background, and other characteristics that are not directly related to what the person has done or will ever do.

There is no society that is completely ascribed or completely achievement oriented. Ascription can be reached by success (reputation) and success can be achieved thanks to the initial "kick" that a favored background can provide. But what Trompenaars signals as the main difference is where status originates, or more specifically, what determines recognition and chances for growth in different societies.

Origins of the social preferences for either ascription or achievement can be multiple. Generally speaking, in environments where change is paramount it is widely understood that those who are younger or at least not too used to old ways of doing things will tend to be privileged, as their capacity to invent and create is supposed to be greater. Inversely, societies where ways of acting have been proven to be efficient and change could only be perceived as an unjustified potential source of risk, seniors or members of groups considered to be a safer option will receive privileges over more diverse alternatives.

The cultural tendency to act more on the achieving or the ascribing side will certainly determine business practices. For instance, delegation is more likely to occur in achieving cultures, promotion will be mostly linked to seniority in ascribed societies, and recruitment and selection will be more likely to be attached to stereotypes in ascribed cultures than in achieving ones.

Emotionals Versus Neutrals

Trompenaars and Hampden-Turner developed a framework called neutrals versus emotionals. According to their data, there would be cultures in which people keep their feelings carefully controlled and subdued. In other cultures, people are called upon to laugh, smile, make gestures, and show feelings.

It is important to understand is that the amount of emotion that people show comes from convention. It does not necessary reflect the level of feelings. Emotionals tend to think that neutrals are cold or that they lack feeling. This may not be the case. They are just brought up not to show how they feel all the time. Neutrals sometimes have the impression that emotionals are immature or uncivilized, because they overrespond or overreact to situations.

Neutrals sometimes have problems trusting emotionals in serious or important tasks because they fear irrational reactions or lack of "cold blood" when needed. Emotionals have problems trusting neutrals because they hide their inner thoughts and therefore they are perceived as "poker faced" or "fake." Emotionals fear unexpected reactions and backstabbing from neutrals.

This framework is often confused with Edward Hall's[3] high versus low context. In fact, they are complementary. Emotionals can be either from high or low context cultures depending on whether they express their feelings directly or indirectly. Neutrals can similarly be from either high or low context cultures. The following table produces some examples.

How we express our feelings	How we express our feelings		
		Directly (low context)	Indirectly (high context)
	Vividly (emotionals)	USA	Latin
	Discreetly (neutrals)	South-East Asian	Scandinavian

For example, a Latin American, a North American, a South East Asian, and a Scandinavian would tell you that he or she is not interested in going to the movies with you this afternoon in very different ways.

An American would say something like "Oh man, thank you for asking. Unfortunately, I will have to say no this time. You see I am so, so, so, so tired…. But it is great that you've invited me. Cheers man!! Don't overdo it with the popcorn, he he!!!"

A Latin American would say something like "Ohhhh, that is sweet!!! Great!!!! I would like to spend the afternoon with you, but are you sure the reviews are very good? Besides, I have this item I have been dreaming of buying for so long… wait, why don't we just go shopping first and then go to the movies?" And then the person who suggested going to the cinema will understand the message, go shopping instead, and not bring up the movie again as a sign of politeness.

A South East Asian would say "Oh, cinema, great, I have seen another movie like that once, I really enjoyed it, it was nice. The theatre you are suggesting is really nice, I have also been there another time, it is great. My brother saw that movie and loved it. The actor looks really much younger than he really is and perhaps he will soon get divorced from his wife because, yes, I never thought it was a good couple… mmm… Yeah let's see… oh, my sister is calling me, please would you give me a second, I will come back in a while…" And then disappear…

A Scandinavian would just say "Thanks, but I do not feel like going to the movies this afternoon."

Using This Information

Trompenaars' frameworks provide extra dimensions to the original views by Geert Hofstede. Knowing about them may allow businessmen to enrich their views and perceptions on international partners, which should help them succeed in their interactions by the correct anticipation of reactions and maximization of opportunities that those unfamiliar with such reactions could rarely predict.

Exercises

1. Imagine a business situation in which partners from external locus of control cultures have to deal with counterparts from internal locus of control societies. Describe the situation and present with avenues of potential resolution.

2. Why do you think diffuse people think that asking personal questions can be considered normal, even in business whereas specifics may think that gathering information on personal aspects of business partners is a waste of time?

CHAPTER 4

Other Frameworks for Cultural Analysis

Contextualizing Background Information

Besides Geert Hofstede and Fons Trompenaars, other authors have developed theories in which they present frameworks for cultural analysis. The classifications originate in the social sciences and some of them are far more dated than the ones produced by business anthropologists. Even if it has never been explicitly acknowledged, most of the frameworks used in business derive from dimensions used in anthropology; therefore, most of the classifications overlap across authors.

The aim of this chapter is to add a few more frameworks to those already developed in previous chapters, in order to present readers with the most complete overview on dimensions for cultural analysis.

In subsequent chapters we will use these dimensions as tools to describe, predict, analyze, and comment on intercultural behaviors occurring in international business.

Frameworks for Cultural Analysis by Major Authors

The chart below lists different frameworks for cultural analysis by different authors. This classification can be useful to identify the dimensions that have not been covered either by Hofstede or by Trompenaars and to develop on them. In most cases, all authors have given similar names to similar frameworks, but there are cases in which they have not. For example, Trompenaars' diffuse versus specific dimension was called space public versus space private by Adler, and space (personal/physical) by Hall. Another example is Adler's being/doing, which carries the same significance as achievers/ascribers by Trompenaars.

Authors	Frameworks
Schein[1]	Relationship with nature Human activity Human nature Relationships with people Time Truth and reality
Trompenaars[2]	Relationship with nature Relationships with people Universalism versus particularism Individualism versus collectivism Affectivity Diffuse versus specific Achievement versus ascription Relationship with time
Kluckhohn and Strodtbeck[3]	Relationship with time Human activity Human nature Relationships with people Time
Adler[4]	Human nature Relationship with nature Individualist versus collectivist Human activity (being versus doing) Space (private versus public) Time (past, present, future)
Hall[5]	Space (personal/physical) Time (monochromic/polychromic) Language (high context, low context) Friendships
Hofstede[6]	Uncertainty avoidance Power distance Individualism versus collectivism Masculinity versus femininity

From the above table, it is possible and easy to identify which frameworks still remain to be treated.

Frameworks for Cultural Analysis and the Authors Who Developed on Them

	Trompe-naars	K and S	Adler	Hofstede	Hall	Schein
Relationship with nature	X		X			X
Relationship with people	X	X			X	X
Universalistic versus particularistic	X					X
Individualist versus collectivist	X		X	X		
Time	X	X	X		X	X
Achievers/ ascribers or being/doing or human activity	X	X	X			X
Human nature		X	X			X
Diffuse versus specifics	X		X		X	
Emotionals versus neutrals	X					
Uncertainty avoidance				X		
Power distance				X		
Masculinity versus femininity				X		
High versus low context					X	

The table above helps us notice there are two frameworks that are addressed neither by Hofstede nor by Trompenaars. These frameworks are: language (high versus low context), by Edward Hall and human nature (by Schein and Kluckhohn and Strodtbeck).

Language (According to Edward Hall)

Language can certainly become a barrier when dealing cross-culturally, but paradoxically, it is not the highest obstacle to overcome in cases where communication needs to exceed mere formalities. The language barrier in many cases can be easily overcome by means of the actions of a good translator.

Meta-language barriers, on the other hand, are much more complex. They refer to ways in which we express our thoughts and feelings. We have already discussed the emotional versus neutral dichotomy in previous chapters, but this is not the only theme in which cultures may vary. This particular framework relates to differences in what we say and what we mean and how these differences are expressed across cultures.

In an attempt to understand cultural mismatches in communication patterns, Edward Hall has developed a specific framework called high versus low context. People from low context cultures usually say what they mean and they mean what they say. Their communication style is very direct and ambiguities are meant to be minimized, as the key issue is to convey a specific message with concrete information. Clarity is important and also considered the main component of successful exchanges. One could think that communicating with these cultures should be simple, as there are supposed to be no hidden meanings, but to high context cultures such an approach to exchanges comes across as aggressive and pushy, almost disrespectful.

In high context cultures which are also external locus of control oriented, it could be considered as "arrogant" to assume that one can determine a fact, put it into words, and convey it to someone else, as reality is quite hard to ascertain and to define in particular words. In other high context cultures, like in the UK in particular, politeness is important and playing a game of understandings and sub-understandings can be considered as a sign of refinement and sophistication. In general, conflict is to be avoided by all means in high context cultures, therefore frontal expressions of views or feelings without sugarcoating are to be avoided.

In low context cultures people use words more than any other tool to communicate. In high context cultures words are just a tool amongst others: people communicate as well by producing situations, through their appearance, with tonalities of voice, with symbols, and with gestures. Harmony, politeness, and keeping the relationship going are considered as keys to success (which is more likely to be obtained through diplomacy than through fighting), so it is very important never to hurt feelings. Words sometimes can be crude, therefore it is tacitly agreed that keeping them to a minimum could be a healthy option and socially satisfactory.

A scheme representing rhetorical styles commonly used in different cultures can be found at http://www.immi.se/intercultural/nr6/pistillo.htm (see Fig. 1 Context ranking of cultures[7]).

Whereas in some cultures it is important to "pass the message with no ambiguity," in others "to save face and save other people's face" takes priority. Being too direct could be perceived as insulting or barbarian in high context cultures. It might mean that there is no interest in pursuing the relationship. In private relations, it can be hurtful and nasty.

In North American, Germanic, and Scandinavian cultures, people prefer to communicate directly. In Latin cultures, it is customary to use a more indirect way of communication, and South East Asians prefer a very indirect "beat-around-the-bush" style.

To the question "Would you like to go to the cinema with me today," a person willing to decline the invitation would communicate their decision in very different ways.

A Scandinavian or a Swiss would simply tell the bare truth: "No, thanks, I shall not go to the cinema with you this time because I do not feel like watching a movie today," a South American would probably respond: "Oh, I'd love to go to the cinema with you, but I feel really tired, I have been taking this new medicine that knocks me down, it is a real pain! Please do ask me next time, I would be delighted!" A South East Asian would probably need more words to express a negative: "Oh! How nice, the cinema, do you remember last time we went, yes, how nice it was, oh, thanks for the invitation, so beautiful of you to do so, but ah, yes, perhaps I shall go, did you ask Susan if she wanted to go with you as well, I know she really wanted to watch that movie you are suggesting, with such a good actress in it...." (and then never go).

Figure 4.1 illustrates the different ways in which people from different cultures have a tendency to communicate. Whereas Scandinavians and

North Americans, Northern Europeans (non-UK) = « to the point »	Latin American, Latin European, UK = « I'm getting to the point »	South-East Asian = « there is no point to get to ».

Figure 4.1. Rhetorical styles across cultures.

other Northern Europeans have a preference to "get to the point" or "focus on the nitty gritty straight away", Latinos prefer to sugarcoat their messages, in particular if these have a negative component. In Asian cultures, the context is very important, but relationships are even more important that the point of the discussion may never be reached, which is not so crucial.

Rhetorical Styles Potentially Leading to Miscommunication Across Cultures

The following passage describes an interesting example of miscommunication between high and low context cultures.

> A company is just a big team (team defined as "two or more people working together in a common way for a common goal"). Needed are reasoned discussions towards mutually acceptable solutions and frank exchanges of opinions and disagreements. All types of teams, sports, business, or marriage, are only as strong as the ability of team members to cooperate and work together. Teams fail without good communication.
>
> People with experience in alien cultures, through travel or work, know that different cultures do things in different ways. Common examples are giving gifts, who sits where at dinner, and the way cultures use language to communicate.
>
> "Use language" does not mean grammar, pronunciation, or vocabulary. These are called language "skills." By logic it's obvious that a certain degree of language-skills-in-common are necessary for cross-cultural communication, but "skills" are just a beginning, not an end.

Maybe the best way to explain this is to use a situation most people are familiar with: husband wife communication. In my case, though, it's not just a male-female problem, but also a Chinese-Western one. Some background: my (Chinese) wife and I have been married five years, have Master's Degrees, good second-language skills and far-more-than-average experience dealing with people from different cultures. In other words, we should have few problems communicating with each other. How I wish that was true. It's not: we argue more about communication than any five other things.

How could that be? We understand (and love) each other, understand each other's culture, and speak each other's language. Women first: her (common) complaints are "You use Chinese like a Westerner: you are too direct, especially when you ask questions and analyze situations; you use too much logic and not enough feelings; you embarrass people by discussing the good and bad points of their proposal in front of others, you are just too rude and not polite enough." To put that in perspective, my family and long-time Canadian friends continually remark on how much more reserved and less aggressive I've become since living in Asia.

My turn. My wife's English is excellent (better than my Chinese), but I go crazy every time I ask her a direct, yes/no question (something like "Do you think I should do this?"). While she does answer me, only very rarely does she use the words "yes" or "no." Instead, she tells a story (of sorts), and from what she says, and how she says it, and her body language, I must guess her answer. The short reason why is because there are no words for "yes" or "no" in Chinese. Classified as "high context language," Chinese (all dialects, Mandarin, Cantonese, etc.) is designed to maintain harmony at all costs, not to be clear. The goal is communicating negatives without actually saying "no." It works for Chinese, but as it is based on the ability to guess meaning, it is tough for Westerners to master—we don't practice making people guess, and have little problem saying "no" when necessary.

Each culture expects language to be used in a specific way. We all grow up learning the right way to use language. Often called "learning how to be polite," it goes far deeper than just politeness. We learn rules—rules that determine our belief in the right and wrong way to use language. Called the Rules of Communication, they determine how we feel language should be used. Language is but a tool used in culturally specific and unique ways.[8]

Rules of Communication	
Western Rules	**Chinese Rules**
Offer as much information as you can	Try not to disagree openly
Be as truthful as possible	Don't ask difficult questions of people above you
Make what you say important (relevant)	Don't openly show you don't understand something
Don't make people guess your meaning	Communicate negatives in an indirect way
Be brief, orderly, and logical	Keep the conversation smooth
Get to, and keep on, the point	Don't embarrass a person in front of a group
State your opinion (even if you disagree)	If what you say will cause problems, don't say it
Ask questions if you don't understand	Don't disturb the harmony of the situation
Being clear is most important	Politeness is most important

High/Low Context and Other Frameworks for Cultural Analysis

Individualism Versus Collectivism

In collectivist cultures, in which harmony and relationships are to be taken care of, direct, simple, straightforward statements are to be avoided. A straight truth could not only hurt and break links that have taken time to develop; but hurting someone may not just mean that the specific relationship might break up, but also that the network of relationships may be altered.

If someone makes someone else lose face through straight confrontation, this may affect the relationships between families, business partners, guanxi (personal networks and networks of networks, in the Chinese sense of the term), and more. One must be very careful to use the right tone, at the right moment with the right person in collective societies, as the actions of the individual (and his/her words!) have an impact that goes beyond just themselves.

Specifics Versus Diffuse

Individuals from diffuse cultures often communicate using high context because all the areas of their lives are strongly interconnected. A dispute with someone at work will affect all relationships at all levels: village level, country club level, meeting at children's school level... therefore communications have to remain smooth and polite.

In specific cultures what one person thinks of another as a worker has nothing to do with the way he or she is considered as a parent, a neighbor, a citizen, etc. Therefore, direct speech is more frequently used in these cases.

Synchronics Versus Sequentials

In sequential cultures, what happened in the past remains mostly in the past so direct forms of expression are allowed, as the consequences of any sort of vexation would not go far beyond a short time period and there is always the chance to start afresh. In synchronic cultures, much attention is paid to the image left through one's expression as the past is always present, even in the future, so it is important to always give a good impression. Hurting somebody in the present will certainly have an impact in the future.

Human Activity Versus Human Nature (or Achievers Versus Ascribers)

In achievement oriented cultures, signaling errors or communicating directly could be perceived as a useful way to help others in their search for perfection. Information being a key success factor and a valuable asset, it is important to be as clear, concise, and concrete as possible, as this allows not only each person to make sure there is no doubt about "the deal," but it can also be considered as a sign of respect towards those whose decisions would be more accurate if they had all the facts in hand.

In ascribed societies, respect and acknowledgment of the role assigned by the group are a sign of respect and modes of communication should at every moment express the adhesion to the tacit norms and hierarchies. Arriving late to a meeting, for example, could be a way to express that someone is highly ranked, the same way that bringing a lawyer to a negotiation could also be a means to say that trust has not been established yet.

Relationship With Nature
(Internal Versus External Locus of Control)

In external locus of control cultures, it is perceived that human beings cannot master the universe, truth, Nature, or other forces. Therefore, pretending that anything is objective, indisputably truthful, or absolute does not mean much. Being precise on matters relating to life, which is anything but precise does not make sense. What does make sense is harmony and peace, therefore much attention is paid to how things are said, rather than to what is said.

In contrast to that, in internal locus of control cultures, the need to master the universe makes it necessary to provide as much information with as much clarity as possible so that it becomes possible to react to facts with the maximum chance of obtaining the goals set. Therefore, being explicit becomes a sign of respect towards those who would then use the objective information given to proceed in life.

Power Distance

In high power distance societies, rank needs to be acknowledged and reminded at all times, and one very useful way to do that is through implicit communication: private lifts will communicate power the same way that private parking lots would do. Never contradicting the boss in public even if the information that you could be providing him or her on the spot would help him or her do a better job is crucial to survive in this type of societies. Information is hardly ever distributed evenly in these societies, so highly ranked people see no real point in discussing much with subordinates. Communication consists basically in having lower ranked individuals show admiration and respect through signs and symbols and highly ranked ones responding to such actions the same way.

In low power distance societies, information is more likely to flow fast to the key decision makers, so being explicit is usually appreciated.

The Exception to All the Rules: Great Britain

Great Britain appears as an interesting example as this culture challenges all the expected behaviors as explained above. Scoring low in power distance, recognized as internal locus of control oriented, promoting achieving behavior, being individualistic and synchronic; Britain still remains a country that communicates implicitly, even with words (for example, see the table at http://3.bp.blogspot.com/-SPrrw9CrJf8/Tc5eDJkimII/AAAAAAAACYE/KLKNblvj1Bo/s1600/5gxvx-724032.jpg).

It is interesting that even if all Anglo-Saxon cultures tend to share very similar rankings in all frameworks, when it comes to context, results vary significantly showing that the Brits are the only Anglo-Saxons to communicate indirectly. There is something specific in the British way of communication that can be upsetting to foreigners, particularly North Americans, who often consider themselves separated from the British by a common language.

Perhaps a colonial tradition followed by strong waves of immigration has not simply led to the worldwide use of English as the main foreign transactions language. Another collateral consequence of this fact could have been the need to recreate a language inside a language that would work as an internal social cohesion factor. Most societies find language as one of the most important indicators of social inclusion, or of cultural belonging. In the case of the UK, because their national language is so widespread, they had to reinvent many codes so that the "inclusion by exclusion" dynamic can continue to take place and the nation would not be completely left without its main identity shaping characteristic.

Human Nature

The second framework that neither Trompenaars nor Hofstede considered was human nature.

The human nature framework describes what the basic nature of people is understood to be in different cultures. For some, most people are evil and cannot be trusted; therefore they need to be controlled. For others, there are both evil and good people in the world, and therefore it is necessary to investigate people before trusting them. But people can be changed with the right guidance. Finally, there are cultures where people are considered to be good at heart, as they are born good.

The interpretation of humanity in these terms has serious consequences in management. Can employees be trusted or do they need to be followed up? The same occurs at a political level, and the philosophies supporting the notion that evil is natural have justified the use of dictatorial regimes to "restore peace."

Studies like Stanley Milgram's[9] on obedience to authority have shown that under certain circumstances men can hurt those who have not aggressed them. Other theories of universal values (Rokeach, Hofstede, Schwartz) have produced value concepts sufficiently similar to suggest that a truly universal set of human values does exist and that cross-cultural psychologists are close to discovering what they are (Michael D. Hills, University of Waikato, New Zealand). For more information on this upcoming theory, see http://orpc.iaccp.org/index. php?option=com_content&view=article&id=51%3Amichael-d-hills& catid=24%3Achapter&Itemid=2.

In any case, rankings on this framework have not been produced, and therefore it is difficult to develop hypotheses or even to comment on origins, causes, and consequences of these mental programmings.

In the following exercises, we invite readers to reflect on the topic, position cultural groups according to their own experience, and self-evaluate their own conceptions and convictions on the matter.

Using This Information

This chapter explains the remaining frameworks that the latest research in cross-cultural management has produced. They, in conjunction with the ones that we previously used, provide an overall view on cultural differences arising from specific mental programmings.

The understanding of the cultural dimensions by all authors facilitates the understanding, prediction, and interaction with cultural behavior in international business.

Exercises

1. Go to http://www.blogcatalog.com/discuss/entry/human-nature-good-or-evil and comment on the discussions by people participating on this blog.

_____

_____

_____

_____

_____

_____

_____

_____

_____

_____

_____

_____

_____

_____

_____

_____

2. What is your own opinion on the matter? Do you think your opinion is the result of cultural influences playing on you as a person? If so, how? If not, why not?

_____

_____

_____

_____

_____

_____

_____

_____

_____

_____

_____

_____

_____

_____

3. List a few potential consequences for a society of having people who conceive humans as evil/good/in-between.

_____

_____

_____

_____

_____

_____

_____

_____

_____

_____

_____

_____

_____

_____

_____

_____

_____

_____

_____

_____

4. Imagine a dialog between someone from a high context culture and someone from a low context one. Point out potential areas of misunderstanding.

_____

_____

_____

_____

_____

_____

_____

_____

_____

PART III

Cross-Cultural Management in Action

CHAPTER 5

National Culture Versus Corporate Culture

Contextualizing Background Information

In previous chapters we have explored frameworks for cultural analysis that would contribute to the understanding of intercultural behavior in business. In the following chapters we will discuss the effects of culture in different aspects of business.

Corporate culture is the first business aspect on which the parameters previously described have an impact: businesses and companies are social arenas in which people interact through the use of signs and symbols that could be comparable to those used at national level. In this chapter, we will elaborate on the development of these social tools, their links to national culture, and the consequences of culture in business at office level.

Corporate Culture

Groups of people naturally develop their own cultures, meaning a commonality of beliefs, experiences, values, and expectations that make them unique. Their culture is one important defining factor of their own identity, providing with a sense of belonging, self-awareness, and protection.

In order to simplify the study and understanding of main cultural phenomena, authors like Geert Hofstede have based their classifications upon the restriction of cultures to national belonging. The justification for such simplification makes sense, as inhabitants of the same country in general share the same history, are exposed to the same media, respect the same laws, and have to adapt to similar situations. Such homogeneization, deriving from the sharing of a common space, can explain why people from the same country could in most cases be identified with a common culture.

But as Hofstede himself puts it, national culture is not the only type of culture that exists, as habits commonly accepted in countries are not the only "acculturating" factor we are exposed to. In fact, we are also the result of the influence of other groups we belong to, such as our generation, religion, profession, and others.

Similarly, companies have their own cultures, which are different from those of other companies. The same way we talk about French culture, we could also talk about McDonald's culture or IBM culture. What we will discuss in this chapter is the influence of this particular acculturating factor: corporate culture.

According to Edgar Schein,[1] corporate culture (or organizational culture) is

> a pattern of basic assumptions that a given group has invented, discovered or developed in learning to cope with its problems of external adaptation and internal integration, that has worked well enough to be considered valid and therefore good to be instructed to new members as the correct way to perceive, think, and feel in relation to these problems.

The definition of corporate culture, in this sense, does not radically differ from that of national culture, apart from the level of analysis. Authors have defined models that characterize corporate culture, whereas others have questioned its existence or at the very least its relevance.

In the following section we will explore different models of corporate culture. Some will assume this factor appears on its own as the result of corporate living. Others will go so far as to deny it, arguing that corporate culture is just a projection of national culture.

Models to Define and Describe Corporate Culture

The Circular Development of Cultural Patterns

The circular development of cultural patterns model by Hunsaker and Cook[2] presents a good explanation on how the corporate culture of an organization is created and constantly reinforced.

Four different components constitute this model and contribute to the sustainability of a set of values that once shared by participants will grant the organization an identity which will comprise and reunite its most particular and personifying characteristics. These elements are: beliefs, norms, data, and analysis.

Beliefs

The model indicates that organizations will develop shared appreciations on what they consider as acceptable or nonacceptable, good or bad, desirable or nondesirable. These common convictions can have as an origin the vision of the founder, characteristics of the market, even the national culture of the country in which the company was created. For example, Facebook culture would suggest that everyone should maximize their capacity to be creative, and therefore smart dressing or formalities that other companies like a Swiss private bank for instance would appreciate as key to communicate seriousness or professionalism, would be naturally rejected. Beliefs in this sense are common values shared by those sharing corporate culture and they contribute to the development of a uniform conception of what is right or wrong to do, what is acceptable and what is not, and what is desirable and what is not.

Norms

Beliefs are usually formalized and institutionalized through the establishment of norms of conduct. These norms can be written in corporate documentation or perhaps even not written at all, but they are in any case shared by those included in the group. Knowing and respecting the norms is a sign of integration to the group. For example, a norm could be that it is acceptable to share aspects of private life in the office, or that it is not. Another norm could be that everyone is expected to have lunch with the other members of his or her department every day.

Data

Norms need to be reinforced in order to be considered as valid. Data means that in the collective memory of the members of the culture, there must be examples of times in which norm infringement was punished and/or the fact that they were respected was saluted. For example, if everyone remembers the time a colleague received a warning because he came to work without a tie, the norm on dress code gets reinforced and its validity is updated.

Analysis

Once data appears, members of the corporate culture start talking about what happened; they analyze facts and make links between norms and data. For example, they assume that coming to work without formal attire is wrong and that it is important to respect this rule (probably because there was much gossip around that fact). They may also seek justification for the norm and project conclusions to other situations, cases, and/or scenarios.

The analysis of data having occurred as a consequence of the respect/ disrespect of the norms, which are based on beliefs, actually supports those beliefs, making corporate culture even stronger. Corporate culture evolves and solidifies through time, as the pattern of circular reinforcement takes place in the shared subconsciousness of the group.

The model in Figure 5.1 is in fact the same as the culture stability model presented in chapter 1 (Figure 1.2) to describe the development and self-reinforcement of national culture. Values at national level are the equivalent of beliefs at corporate culture level. The idea of circular reinforcement is what is very specific to these two models.

Geert Hofstede and the Nonexistence of Corporate Culture

Geert Hofstede,[3] the famous business anthropologist, presents a very controversial view on corporate culture in his 1999 article in the academic journal *Organizational Dynamics*, in which he predicts what management in the twenty-first century would look like.

In this publication, Hofstede denies the existence of corporate culture as a set of values, but only understands it as a series of practices that can be imposed by management through the use of power channels, but that will not be the result of natural processes being generated from inside the organization by its members.

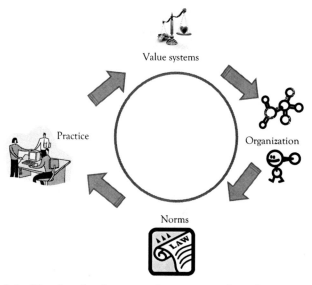

Value systems

Practice

Organization

Norms

Figure 5.1. Circular development of corporate cultural patterns.

According to Hofstede, national culture generates and determines values that are already hardwired in the minds of people by the age of 12 and these values would never change from then on. Therefore, a company cannot shape beliefs or values. An organization can only ask employees and management to act upon rules originated in values that are not necessarily their own. This is a main conceptual difference from the Hunsaker and Cook's model, in which beliefs are generated within the organization. In Hofstede's model, they are not, particularly when companies go global or at least international and need to impose uniformity in their operational routines.

For example, a multinational corporation with headquarters in a country with low power distance may have decided that it is good practice to have regional managers institute an open door policy in their offices. This habit may have been the result of beliefs that have turned into norms and then been analyzed, accepted, and reinforced by the local corporate/national culture. When this company internationalizes and attempts to take this practice abroad, issues may come up. The policy can be rejected, ignored, or a hybrid of the practice may be put in place, such as a series of managers who do not close their doors, but make it clear to everyone that it is not well perceived to show up unannounced. Or else the local culture will generate a different practice on the side, which will serve as a message to everyone about power and who really holds it.

Hofstede's perspective still brings an extra item to the debate. Practices can be imposed by organizations, but these will not affect values. They will be superficially accepted and can be assumed, but in some way, they will end up acting as yet a new way the local community will have found to express their true beliefs and preferred ways of operating.

Postings on Facebook are an interesting example of how a practice can be globalized, whereas people from different cultures will use it according to their own meanings and values. "Friends" from emotional cultures, in which sharing feelings is accepted and even encouraged, will use Facebook to express how they feel and will be very explicit in their displays of emotions. Other cultures will use the same tool as an opportunity to show wit or just to relay facts, share music preferences, etc. In this case, no matter how global the tool and the practice can be, the values remain still very much anchored in the inborn national culture.

The scientific background that Hofstede uses as argument to support his particular point of view lies in the research by Philippe d'Iribarne,[4] who studied three different plants of the same industrial corporation in three different locations. In 1980, d'Iribarne compared management in three technically identical production plants of a French-owned aluminum company: one in France, one in the USA, and the third in the Netherlands.

d'Iribarne's observations concluded that each plant would be managed according to values that could be related to each of the national cultures of the countries in which they were located. The interactions between people in the three locations followed different logics that coincided with what would be expected as behavior occurring in the countries in which they operated rather than with values that could have been generated from a corporate culture created by the organization and then conveyed to everyone involved anywhere in the world.

For instance, in France, where high power distance prevails and there is high uncertainty avoidance, relationships were conducted under the logic of honor. It was a class mini-society, with at least three levels divided by antagonism, but linked by respect. Hierarchy was perceived as a means to preserve honor. In the USA, on the other hand, what prevailed was the logic of fair contract. With low uncertainty avoidance and low power distance, plus high levels of individualism and masculinity, the generalized rule was "let the best one win." And therefore all relationships were ruled by negotiations and the shared acceptance that all parts were interdependent on each other. In feminine Netherlands, relationships were based on compromise, and relationships were non-antagonist. Conflict was solved through lengthy discussions and decision-making was based on generalized agreements.

Hofstede's perception leaves little hope for the predicted changes in the world map following globalization, which would foresee the world as organized not according to the current political division, but on networks, economic power, distribution of income, capital, labor, entrepreneurship, knowledge, and corporate risk. It is difficult to understand international operations in which most people have to work in contradiction to their own values, but compelled by imposed practices that do not result from their own traditional response to the environment. On the other hand, the success of international media programs to a similar extent all over the world would suggest that there are common patterns shared by everyone on the planet and that this could be a good start for homogenization of patterns, if there was such a need.

Fons Trompenaars and the Four Main Typologies of Corporate Culture

A second business anthropologist, Fons Trompenaars, developed a model based on power distance and person versus task orientation. Four typologies result from this crossing, allowing the classification of four different types of corporate culture behaviors.

Even if these typologies are not necessarily based on national culture exclusively, because the criteria that defines them could also be attributed to other factors, such as the nature of an industry, the kind of product or service provided, the historical moment of the foundation, and so forth, still there is a strong link between each one of the types of corporate cultures and the national cultures in which these tend to prevail.

Figure 5.2 outlines a scheme to synthesize the four main types of corporate culture according to Trompenaars.

CORPORATE CULTURES

We examine Corporate Culture through crossing dimensions: equality/hierarchy and person/task orientations.

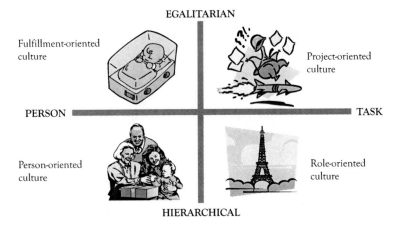

Figure 5.2.

According to the level of hierarchy and to the orientation (either task based or person based) of the organization, corporate cultures can fit into one of the following four types: the family culture (hierarchical and person-oriented), the Eiffel tower culture (role oriented and hierarchical), the missile culture (task oriented and egalitarian), and the incubator (person oriented and of low power distance).

The **Family Culture**, as described by Trompenaars, would be one characterized by a paternalistic management style, where promotion is granted to a great extent by seniority and in which long-term relationships between the institution and its members are valued. In this type of culture, one does more than what the contract establishes and people appreciate the pleasure derived from harmonious relationships between employees and employers. Pleasing superiors is considered as an important advantage and pressure is moral and social, rather than financial or legal. The loss of affection, recognition, or "a place within the family" can even be considered as a form of punishment in itself.

The **Eiffel Tower Culture**, even if also hierarchically established, does not find in relationships the structure for its own functioning, but in a set of rules that are pre-established and that constitute the essence of the labor contract. In fact, the Eiffel Tower culture consists basically in the bureaucratic division of labor with various roles and functions prescribed in advance. Power and functions are allocated and coordinated in a top-down manner. The origin and justification of authority in this type of corporate culture comes from the occupancy of a role. And respect is due to the role, not to the person occupying it. The main objective of this system is to make it as impersonal as it could possibly be, making it one in which everyone is subordinate to rules and those rules determine a hierarchy that will make sure they are followed. Managers have power, but only because rules determine that he or she is the power holder.

The **Guided Missile Culture**, characterized by low power distance and action orientation, is defined around one very specific aim: to catch the customer. Relationships are temporary and based on the need to cooperate on specific projects, as opposed to a means to develop trust. Achievement is celebrated and sometimes the objective justifies the means. Hierarchy is perceived as an obstacle that prevents fast reactions and has to be avoided, but on the other hand, the combination of a Guided Missile structure with an Eiffel Tower one could produce a matrix structure, which could be deemed most appropriate in certain cases. Change is fast in this type of culture, as it happens every time the target moves, which is virtually all the time. Turnover is high in general, and loyalty to projects and professions is higher than loyalty to companies.

The **Incubator Culture**, which is both personal and equalitarian, is in general a short-term one, as the fulfillment of individuals prevails over the organization. In general there is no structure or very little structure, as these are small organizations. Examples of incubators include: doctors in group practice, legal partners, consultants, and so forth. In general, as soon as these companies grow, they call for other types of structure, which naturally calls for new corporate cultures more appropriate to their shape and form.

As mentioned above, Trompenaars does not link the type of corporate culture exclusively to a national culture, but he does signal national culture characteristics as the main origin for each one of these types of culture. Industry type can certainly have an influence on the type of corporate culture that will develop. For instance, a bank will most probably align with an Eiffel Tower corporate culture, rather than with a Guided Missile Culture and this no matter where the bank is located. Similarly, an IT company would rather need to organize as a Guided Missile or an incubator, in order to be able to quickly respond to the needs of the market before competitors do and to be at the forefront of innovation.

Conclusion

The debate on whether corporate culture exists as such independently from national cultures is ongoing. Culturalists may support the fact that management being mainly a cultural activity, it will not greatly evolve through time because cultures do not greatly evolve through time either.

Reality shows that with globalization there is a need for uniformization of practices across borders, which may be restrictive of the natural expression of people at work, and may perhaps lead to frustration and even to the imposition of practices that would not necessarily be the most effective or the best for each case.

Concrete cases like McDonald's amongst thousands of others demonstrate that a brand can carry with it the signature of a particular corporate culture and that aligning with it may be symbolic of agreement with at least practices that are global (if not with values that are global).

Hofstede's view on the nonexistence of such a thing as corporate culture leads one to wonder whether international management is even possible, as he remains very firm in his idea that multinational organizations stand for values that originated in their home country and that will not be shared equally with their employees and managers from other national origins. Would in this case the mere sharing of practices be enough or will this be a very frustrating scenario in which some regret working halfheartedly in an environment they find is imposed on them rather than the result of a natural state of affairs?

The Elements of Corporate Cultures

Four distinctive elements define corporate cultures. These are:

- Values
- Role models
- Habits
- Communication patterns

Values express the philosophy of a company and provide guidelines for directing behavior. They synthesize what people working for or relating to a specific company believe in. The stronger the values and the most widely shared, the stronger the corporate culture.

Role models are the personification of the values shared by people working for the specific company in question. A role model is someone that everyone in the company relates to as a hero. Role models need not be alive. A role model could be the founder of the company, or an eminent character who once worked at it. A role model could also be an employee whose behavior typifies success norms (for example the person who managed to increase sales by a third thanks to the development of a new market), or the celebrity researcher who published a book that brought the whole department of a faculty worldwide recognition.

Habits are activities that take place on a regular basis and that serve as opportunities to reinforce the fact that employees belong to or are part of the culture of an institution. Habits can be formal or informal and include the morning coffee shared by members of a department, the annual Christmas celebration, or taking a pint at the pub as a group after work. Rituals favor communication amongst members and reinforce ties.

Communication patterns are defined as the formal and informal social links and means of expression and feedback that take place within an organization. Formal communication can take place through e-mail, memos, letters, reports, and also through meetings, formal speeches, and newsletters. Informal communication networks include friendships at work, corridor gossip, grapevines, anecdotes, shared stories, and so forth.

Now You Tell Us...

How do you think the elements of corporate culture can be altered by management in order to increase profitability?

Food for Thought...

In the past, when all employees of a company needed to "go to work" in order to join the means of production (e.g., machinery), it was easy to identify and moderate the culture of a company, simply because people saw each other and shared spaces more frequently and on a regular basis.

Nowadays, technology permits distance working and therefore relationships are affected. How do you think new ways of working are altering corporate cultures and the way they develop? Google "Location independent working" and write a few lines on the future of corporate culture once patterns have been altered.

And the Consultant's View...

Consultants from the firm McKinsey have developed a framework for analysis, which is called "The 7-S" framework. This tool allows consultants to make a fast and effective assessment of the company taking into consideration the main factors that, when interacting in a holistic way, constitute a running company (for an image of the model, see http://www.mindtools.com/media/Diagrams/mckinsey.jpg).

These factors are:

- **Shared values**: They constitute the core of the company's beliefs. They keep people together. They give meaning to what the whole group is striving for. In general, these shared values are formalized in the corporate mission statement.
- **Strategy**: Plan to reach established goals.
- **Structure**: Establishes how power and resources are allocated, distributed, and administered.
- **Systems**: Processes and routines indicating how the work should be done.
- **Staff**: Type of personnel and their qualities, capacities, and qualifications.
- **Style**: Managerial way of having things done (participative, authoritative, charismatic, etc.)
- **Skills**: Know-how of the organization.

According to the model, consultants tend to try to change "hard factors" (strategy, structure, and systems) when they try to produce change in the culture of a company. What they often forget is that the soft factors, which are harder to identify (superordinate goals, skills, staff, and style) are the ones that require real input for sustained and sustainable change.

And Now You...

Extend your research on the 7-S framework and determine why the soft factors are more difficult to identify whereas they are the most important to deal with in order to produce sustained and sustainable change.

Using This Information

The understanding of what influences and impacts corporate culture is key to manage subsidiaries abroad. Through a well-generated, strongly reinforced corporate culture it becomes quite easy to disseminate homogeneous practices across countries and overcome deceptive negative reactions from diverse stakeholders when trying to get people to use and perform certain duties and tasks.

Whether corporate culture exists or not, practices are in any case a key component of managerial life and of corporate life in general, therefore it is very convenient to find a way to design processes that facilitate the development and use of the most effective tools in a similar way wherever and whenever required.

CHAPTER 6

Cross-Cultural Communication

Ming Li and Veronica Velo

Contextualizing Background Information

Communication is probably the main issue in cross-cultural matters. Conflict, loss of trust, bureaucracy, delays, good deals going wrong, and many other deceptive situations are the direct consequence of poor communication in international business.

The aim of this chapter is to discuss the communication process in detail, suggest ways in which it should be improved, and present examples of why and how bad communications practice could be as damaging as good communication could be rewarding.

Communication

Communication has been defined in numerous ways, including: "The process by which people share information, meanings and feelings through the exchange of verbal and nonverbal messages,"[1] or "The act of transmitting messages, including information about the nature of the relationship, to another person who interprets these messages, and gives them meaning."[2]

We can present the communication process as shown in Figure 6.1. This model assumes the sender and the receiver have the same cultural background. The cultural field refers to those culturally based elements of a person's background that influence communication, for example: education, values, attitudes, and so forth.

Figure 6.1 shows that every communication has a message *sender* and a message *receiver*. Both the sender and the receiver play an active role

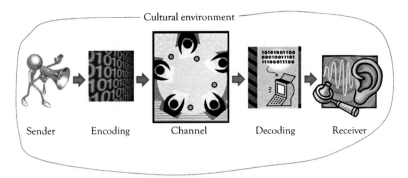

Figure 6.1. Monocultural communication process.

in the communication process. As ideas, feelings, or information cannot be communicated directly, people must symbolize them for expression. Therefore, *encoding* describes the production of a symbol message (words or behaviors) from the sender; this *message* is sent through some *channel* (letter, phone, face to face meeting, etc.), and *decoding* describes the process by which the receiver interprets a meaning from the symbol message.

Some key features of communication:

- Successful communication requires not only that the message is transmitted but also that it is understood.
- The message sent by the sender is never identical to the message received. Distortion can occur at all stages of the communication process.
- Communication occurs in a context; culture is often one important context. To achieve understanding between the sender and the receiver, a vast amount of common information needs to exist between the two.
- Communication is irreversible, once a message is sent, it cannot be taken back.
- Communication is a dynamic process between the sender and the receiver.

In intracultural communications, the context facilitates the interaction, as collective mental programming has set up the terms of the exchange even between individuals who had never met before. The shared ideas received during a similar socialization process on what is good/bad, desirable/undesirable, acceptable/nonacceptable are taken as a given and therefore there is a minor degree of effort to be made in order to understand the message. Even the system of coding and decoding is alike when dealing intraculturally. People use the same symbols (channels) to express the same emotions or messages; for example, what you would normally say via e-mail in one culture, you could prefer to express in person in another, whereas with people from similar backgrounds, this difference does not appear as such.

Monocultural communication is conducted through seeking *similarity*. Common language, behavioral patterns, and values from the same cultural background allow people to predict the response of others to certain kinds of messages, and react appropriately based upon this prediction. This almost tacit understanding is illustrated in the two conversations conducted between two Americans and two Chinese in Box 6.1.

Cross-cultural communication happens when a person from one culture sends a message to a person from another culture. In other words, the sender and the receiver have different cultural fields. Languages, behavior patterns, and values are different in each culture. The encoded message is determined by the communication skills, knowledge, and culture of the

Box 6.1

American 1: I am visiting my boyfriend in Chicago this weekend.

American 2: Wow! That sounds like a romantic plan! Good for you!

American 1: Yes! It will be fun. But I cannot take my cat with me, would you mind feeding it for three days?

American 2: Sure. No problem, I've got the key to your place.

American 1: Thank you so much!

Chinese 1: I am going to Shanghai this weekend, to see Wei Yu.

Chinese 2: Oh, great! Please send my regards to him! Such a great boyfriend, isn't he?

Chinese 1: Yes, he certainly does think very highly of you as well.

Chinese 2: Who is taking care of Xiao Xiao (the cat)? Please let me feed him, he is so cute!

Chinese 1: Are you sure it's not too much trouble?

Chinese 2: It's my pleasure!

sender. The symbols that people use to express an idea are different. The preference and mode of using different communication channels vary in different cultures. Receivers from different cultures also interpret the same message differently. Thus, overall, culture influences each stage of cross-cultural communication. The fact that the sender and the receiver are from different cultures means that they have less common information to share, less tacit understanding, and so more distortion can be present during the communication process.

One of the "rules of the game" that appears as quite obvious from the messages above indicates what is expected as a reaction from a friend and also what is considered as "polite behavior" and what is not both in China and in the USA.

In China, it is polite to offer help to a friend, even if he or she has not asked for it directly. Actually, it would be impolite not to do so. Further, it would seem very impolite to ask for help directly. In the USA, it is expected that a friend would ask for help if needed, so the potential provider of this help does not think he or she needs to volunteer unless asked to do so.

The context in this case clearly indicates what is expected/not expected from someone else; it also indicates what is polite/not polite to do. When dealing intraculturally, the rules of communication are shared, which is not always the case when dealing interculturally.

If the American 1 in the example above was having a conversation with the Chinese 2 person, the latter might have felt a bit shocked to be asked for help so directly. He would have preferred having the American continue the conversation for a bit longer until he had been given time to volunteer to offer the support as a way to underline the importance of their friendship. By asking directly for help, the American seems impatient, intolerant, and even perhaps interested in using the Chinese to do something he could be doing himself.

If Chinese 1 in the example above was having this conversation with American 2, on the other hand, he would be extremely disappointed to see that the American character would not be volunteering to take him to the airport. He would come across as insensitive, not interested in pursuing the friendship, and very selfish (in particular if Chinese 1 has done favors for him in the past). This would in fact have been a big misunderstanding,

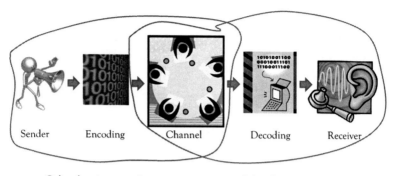

Sender   Encoding   Channel   Decoding   Receiver

Cultural environment 1   Cultural environment 2

Figure 6.2. Cross-cultural communication process.

as the American character would probably have been eager to give a hand to the Chinese, had he asked for help directly.

We can see through these examples how communicating can be easier monoculturally, as the cultural field acts a facilitator in the encoding, decoding, and the choice of the channel.

But things may get a bit more complicated when dealing cross-culturally, as shown in Figure 6.2.

Indeed, culture may affect communication at every level of the process.[3]

The Sender

The sender carries within his own background a set of norms about how to behave. In the previous case, it includes his or her own notion on what is agreeable to ask and what is not, what is desirable or not, what is offensive and what is not, what is appropriate and what is not, and so forth. Many factors influence these notions or perceptions, and not all of them are cultural. Some of them are just psychological. But what is undeniable is that whereas American 1 above would have considered it fine to demand a ride, Chinese 1 would have never thought so. The message being deployed by the two characters is therefore consistently different.

Encoding

The choice of words, gestures, attitudes, actions... to communicate is culturally sensitive. In the example above, Chinese 1 chose not to ask for help directly, but he did convey all the "hints" that were needed in order to have the message come across in his culture. The American encoding was much simpler and more direct: the person who needed a favor just asked for it straightforwardly.

Channel

We do not know very much about the channel used in the examples above to convey the message. The Americans were probably doing it anywhere: a bar, the office, in the parking lot, in the staff room next to the water bottle, on the bus... In contrast, in order to make sure that Chinese 2 would "get the message," Chinese 1 has probably given much thought to how to make sure he could have Chinese 2 offer assistance without having to ask for it. They are probably at a restaurant and Chinese 2 will offer to pay for the meal; or perhaps the timing was right: Chinese 1 owed a favor to Chinese 2 and this was just the time to give a hint on how to pay back for it. In any case, the tools used to convey the message were very similar.

Decoding

Understanding meaning is also cultural, so what each of us understands from others is highly influenced by our backgrounds. In the case above, unless American 1 had explicitly asked for a favor, American 2 would have probably not offered it. In his cultural context, if someone needs a favor, he or she must ask for it. If there is no request, then there is no need. In China, on the other hand, there is a different tacit communication rule: it is rude and pushy to ask for a favor directly. Therefore, when a Chinese sees that a friend to whom he/she owes a favor suggests he/she may be in need of help, the natural reaction is to offer support.

The Receiver

The same way a sender is influenced by his own culture when developing and expressing a message, so is the receiver. The latter will subconsciously pick the portions of the original ideas that have not been lost in the previous phases of communication according to what was learnt during the socialization process.

Misunderstanding can also occur easily in cross-cultural communication due to many sources, including, but not limited to:

1. Misperception: cultures act as filters and lead us to distort, block, and even create what we choose to see and to hear.
2. Misinterpretation (or misattribution): occurs when individuals give wrong meaning to observations and their relationships. Based on our experience and culture, we make assumptions about what we perceive so we will not have to rediscover meanings each time we encounter similar situations. These assumptions may not be right, and assumptions held by individuals are different because their experience and cultures are different. One cause of misinterpretation is *stereotyping*. Stereotyping is a form of categorization that organizes our experience and conditions our behavior towards various groups within society.
3. Misevaluation: evaluation involves judging whether someone or something is good or bad. We use our own culture as a standard of measurement, reflexively judging that which is like our own culture as normal and good and that which is different as abnormal and bad.

Case study

Here in Box 6.2 is one case of a miscommunication between an American school director and a Greek lecturer around the delivery of the grades.

In the American manager's mind, the employee was supposed to make an accurate estimation of how long the job would take, with perhaps a few days extra of precautionary cushion in order not to be put out of schedule by unexpected delays. Therefore, when the manager asked how much it would take and the employee responded 10 days, he assumed it would be very generous to give him an extra 50% time, and that because of that understanding offer, the report would have been ready when agreed.

In the Greek employee's mind, things do not work that way. For him, the boss should have known that the actual time the job would require was about a month. Because of power distance, the superior is supposed

Box 6.2

American: "How long will it take you to finish the marking?"

Greek: "It all depends, how long do you think it should?"

American: "Well, you produced the exam papers, so you should know."

Greek: "10 days."

American: "OK. Let's then say two weeks, so that we know for sure they will be ready by then"

In fact, the amount of marking was huge and could never have been finished in 10 days. Two weeks later, nevertheless, the lecturer is almost ready because he has worked days and nights and has been extremely productive. But he still needs an extra day to wrap things up.

American: "Where are the grades?"

Greek: "They will be in your office by tomorrow."

American: "But we had agreed everything would be ready by today."

The Greek hands in his resignation. The American is surprised.

to know more. He may have been shocked by the answer "I don't know," as that is something one would rarely hear from a highly positioned executive from a high power distance society. By saying he could have finished within 10 days, the employee was intending to show commitment and good intentions, but he never really thought he could make it. He was probably expecting the employer to appreciate his intentions, but to get back to him with a patronizing voice saying, "You are wrong, this will take you 40 days," and then be surprised when the employee would have finalized by day 25.

In the current circumstances, both actors end up disappointed: the Greek character may think his boss is incompetent (he does not even know how much it takes to do the job), incapable of showing empathy (he did not appreciate the efforts made by the employee), and useless at managing the human factor at work. Therefore, he needs to resign in order to punish him and to embarrass him in front of his peers.

The American boss is frustrated because his employee did not meet the deadline. Being from an internal locus of control culture, very universalistic, and from low context, he thinks one has to comply with his promises regardless of the process and the circumstances. He did not consider the fact that most probably a Greek national would find it difficult to confront an authority or to have him lose face in public, therefore his only choice was to leave banging the door.

Communication is effective to the extent to which we can achieve mutual understanding and minimize misunderstanding. Our ability to avoid misunderstandings starts from understanding the challenges of cross-cultural communication. These challenges directly involve the use of verbal language, non-verbal behaviors, and different communication styles across cultures.

Nobody said that communicating cross-culturally would be a walk in the park and it is understandable that many may be frustrated by this and keep being annoyed by other people's choices and decisions. Being a cross-cultural manager does not mean that one will never be disturbed by diversity. Even the most passionate diversity seeker who appreciates variety will at some point wish others would see life through his eyes. But the big difference between a good cross-cultural manager and a parochial one is that the former will be able to enhance his team's creativity to the highest, and will embrace profit.

Linguistic Challenges of Cross-Cultural Communication

One important way of communication is through spoken language. It is estimated that there are more than 2,500 distinct languages currently spoken in the world. Among them, more than 100 are spoken by more than one million people each. The nine languages that have the largest number of native speakers are Mandarin, Spanish, English, Hindi, Arabic, Bengali, Portuguese, and Japanese.[4] To communicate with people from other cultures, there has to be a common language. However, even people who speak the same language but from different countries can be surprised when they hear 'their' language spoken to them in an unfamiliar fashion. For example, "candy" and "elevator" in America are "sweets" and "lift" in Britain respectively. In cross-cultural communication, often one or both (all) of the communicators must use a common second language that is very different from their own.

Use of a second language

Cross-cultural communication is difficult. Even when there is an appropriate medium such as a second language in common (e.g., English as "lingua franca"), understanding is still difficult to come by. The use of a second language presents a number of challenges:

1. Misunderstanding caused by low level of language fluency.
2. It is mentally straining for second-language user.
3. First-language speakers tend to modify their speech by reducing the speed, simplifying the sentence, or adopting "foreigner speak" as in the example shown in Box 6.3.[5]
4. Second-language speakers pretend to understand.
5. People who speak a fluent second language are also regarded as competent in other respects, which is not necessarily true.

Box 6.3

Manager: Miss Li, did you type the corrections to the speech to be given by Mr Wei?

Li: [pause] Sorry, I no understand.

Manager: [In a louder voice] We need to enter the corrections and then send this back to Wei by closing time

Li: Would you like me to send the file back to Mr Wei as it is?

Manager: Miss Li [pause] take speech [pause] Mr Wei [pause] with amendments in

Li: Sorry!

In the case above, the miscommunication is clear. For the Chinese employee, there was a reason not to amend Mr. Wei's speech (most probably Mr. Wei is a superior officer with great connections and correcting him would be an offence—in particular by a younger woman). Li's intention was certainly good and she did understand that her manager wanted her to type the amendments and transport the material to Mr. Wei. But she could just not confront him directly and he felt he needed to avoid conflict. Li was hoping the manager would rethink his order by pretending not to understand it, but what Li did not understand was that no matter how many times her boss repeated the same sentence again and again, things would not move forward because he would just become irritated, and the amendments would in the end have to be made.

If there was a reason for the amendments not to be inserted, the manager would expect his employee to mention it directly instead of using artifacts to distort the meaning. To the American manager, it is paramount that all information that could challenge the good functioning of the company is pointed out in order to be avoided or to prevent further malfunctions. In the mind of the Chinese employee, saving the face of the superior is paramount, but to contradict him is an offence he will try to avoid by all means... so no matter how angry the manager can get by repeating the same sentence over and over again, things may not be any better.

Other Linguistic Considerations

When we speak other languages, it is also important to understand how language is used in different social situations. In most languages, there are nonstandard forms and usages of language that are difficult for second-language speakers to understand. These nonstandard forms of language include the following:

Slang	An informal form of language typically more playful or metaphorical and associated with a particular subgroup.
Jargon	An informal form of language associated with a particular subgroup but often a very specialized or technical language of people engaged in a similar occupation or activity.
Euphemism	The words that by tradition or convention are not often used publicly.
Idioms	Unique ways of combining words to express a particular thought.
Proverbs and Maxims	Short sayings that can be found in all languages, they often reflect espoused values in different cultures and advise people how they should behave.

Differences in Nonverbal Communication Across Cultures

In cross-cultural communication, beyond *what* is being said, *how* it is being said is also important. According to Albert Mehrabian, three elements account for our feelings for the person who puts forward a message: words account for 7%, tone of voice accounts for 38%, and body language accounts for 55%. Nonverbal communication, according to Noller[6] counts for 70% of communication between people in the same language group. Important nonverbal communication includes tone of voice, use of silence, eye contact, facial expression, gestures, conversational distance, and touching, among others.

Tone of Voice

Tone of voice includes pitch, volume, speed, tension, variation, and some other voice qualities such as breathiness or creakiness. Some cultures communicate in higher volume and higher speed than other cultures in normal circumstances. Different cultures ascribe different meanings to features and qualities of tone of voice. For example, in the United States, loud, low-pitched, fast speech indicates dominance; in Germany soft, low-pitched, breathy speech indicates dominance. In addition, these and other features of voice, such as accent, can indicate the cultural identity of the speaker. When communicating with different cultures, people tend to interpret tone of voice based on their own culture.

Silence[7]

Some cultures such as the United States see talk as a more important part of communication, people from these cultures have low tolerance for silence, seeing it as something to be filled with conversation. However, silence is viewed differently in collective cultures such as China and Japan. It is regarded as an important part of communication in these cultures. For example, in Japan, four meanings can be conveyed by silence: truthfulness, social discretion, embarrassment, and defiance. In China, some people treat silence as a virtue, "Silence is golden." In business negotiation, some cultures tend to use talk as a control strategy, and other cultures tend to use silence as a control strategy.

In Latin cultures, silence can usually mean failure to communicate. When taking an elevator or sharing a meal, long silences can be interpreted as boredom or disinterest in others. Words, even meaningless words that fill the space are necessary to make people feel comfortable.

Eye Contact

Different cultures have different norms governing how long people should maintain eye contact during interactions. For example, in the United States, gazing is typically interpreted as a sign of friendliness; persistent gazing is perceived as hostile or aggressive; avoiding eye contact suggests shyness, unfriendliness, and insincerity. However in Africa and some countries in South East Asia, gazing conveys anger; and in Japan, people avoid eye contact, they look instead at people's necks.

Facial Expression

Facial expression is an important way to convey information, especially emotions including anger, fear, sadness, disgust, happiness, and surprise. However, different cultures attach different meanings to the same facial expression. For example, in the United States, smiling is associated with happiness; in Japan, smiling is a sign of hiding displeasure, sorrow, and anger; and in China, smiling sometimes is seen as a lack of self-control and calmness.

Gestures

Different cultures use gestures differently. For example, in most cultures people nod their heads up and down to say "yes," and shake their heads from side to side to say "no". However, in Bulgaria, people do the opposite; they nod their heads up and down to say "no" and shake their heads from side to side to say "yes". Hence, the same gestures can mean very different things in different cultures. Here you can see some of the different meanings of a few gestures:

Tapping side of nose	UK: It's a secret Italy: I'm suspicious
Two-finger salute	UK: Up yours! USA: Victory
Moving hand towards body	UK: Come here Philippines: Go away
Tapping side of forehead	UK: Stupidity Germany: Intelligence
Stamping your foot	UK: Impatience China: Anger

Conversation Distance

Each person has around her or him an invisible bubble of space, which is called personal space. It expands and contracts depending on factors such as the relationship to the people nearby, the person's emotional state or cultural background, and the activity being performed. Few people are allowed to penetrate this personal space and then only for a short period of time. There are four types of conversation distance people keep from each other when they communicate as shown in Figure 8.3. Public distance is used for public speaking, social distance is for interactions among acquaintances, personal distance is for interaction among good friends or family members, and intimate distance is for embracing, touching, or whispering with intimate others. The personal distance standard for Northern Americans is shown in Figure 8.3. According to Hall, different cultures maintain different standards of personal space when talking to each other. Therefore, what is considered as appropriate *conversation distance* differs from one culture to another. In Latin cultures, the relative conversational distances are smaller, and people tend to be more comfortable standing close to each other; in Nordic cultures, the conversational distances are larger, people tend to keep distance from each other. For example, a Spanish businessman and a Danish businessman were talking in a meeting room. While the Spanish businessman kept moving closer to the Danish businessman during the conversation, the Danish man kept backing away from the Spanish man. When the Danish businessman hit the wall, the Spanish businessman realized he was invading the comfortable conversation space of the Danish businessman. Gauging the conversation distance appropriate to different cultures is important so that people don't feel too distant or too close, and such awareness improves cross-cultural understanding.

Touching

People from different cultures use touching behavior differently, if at all, during conversations. In northern Europe one does not touch others. Even the brushing of overcoat sleeves can elicit an apology. Other low-touching cultures include English, Germanic, and Asian. In Mediterranean, Eastern

European, and Arabian cultures, people touch each other frequently during conversation as a sign of closeness, mutual trust, and friendliness.

Communication Styles Across Cultures

Email Exercise

In this exercise you assume the role of the project leader of a team with members located in different countries. You have just learned that one team member, Keiko Suzuki from Japan, has failed to deliver an important due report to the project team as agreed. This is not the first time Keiko has disappointed and not just in her ability to meet deadlines but also the quality of her work. Previously, she provided inaccurate data to another team member who fortunately spotted it before it could become a serious problem. Her poor performance is drawing the attention of other team members and is a risk to keeping the project on track. You decide it is time to address the problem immediately and would prefer to do it over the phone but your previous conversations with Keiko have been strained and left you feeling unsure if she fully understood you. You put this down to the "language barrier" and feel an email would work best in this situation.

Write an email in English to initiate this feedback process in the box below.

To: Keiko Suzuki
From:
CC:
BCC:
Subject:

Now exchange your written email with someone you know and you can both assume the role of Keiko as she reads and reacts to the email. Answer the following:

1. How do you feel after you read this email? Happy? Neutral? Upset? Any other feelings?

    _____

    _____

    _____

    _____

    _____

2. Are you prompted to change your behavior in the future? Why?

    _____

    _____

    _____

    _____

    _____

Using This Information

When you are communicating with people from different cultures:

1. Don't assume that what we mean is what is understood.
2. Don't assume that what you understood is what is meant.
3. Don't assume similarity, even though there are some universal communication behaviors.
4. Use of a second language is challenging.
5. Familiar nonverbal behaviors may have different meanings.
6. Different cultures prefer different communication styles.

Remember: In cross-cultural communication, make sure you know not only *what* to say, but also *how* to say it.

Here are some recommendations for effective cross-cultural communication based on William B. Gudykunst[8] and Stella Ting-Toomy:

1. Be *open*—share part of yourself and be open to the differences of others.

2. *Listen* actively and proactively—actively noticing differences, contexts, and perspectives.

3. Show *empathy*—being sensitive to others' needs and feelings, also communicate that you feel what the other person feels, both verbally and nonverbally. Build rapport.

4. *Respectfulness*—show respect and positive regard for another person.

5. *Tolerate ambiguity*—remain calm, do not become anxious when there is unknown or ambiguous information.

6. *Flexibility*—check and recheck assumptions, shift perspectives, and adapt verbal and nonverbal communications appropriately.

CHAPTER 7

Cross-Cultural Negotiations

In this chapter different negotiation techniques will be explored, as well as ways in which they are used cross-culturally and how these would contribute to the success of an international business.

Assuming that local assumptions, values, expectations, techniques, objectives, and processes are global is wrong, and traveling to do business thinking international partners always operate as locals do is just a one-way ticket to a wrong deal, or worse, to an unaccomplished one.

This chapter helps understand different negotiation techniques, link them to the frameworks for cultural analysis, and develop tools and attitudes towards better business opportunities.

Contextualizing Background Information

The process of a negotiation can be defined in many ways, including "A process in which at least one individual tries to persuade another individual to change his ideas or behaviour," or "A process in which at least two partners with different needs and viewpoints try to reach an agreement on matters of mutual interest." In any case, there are a few defining elements that constitute the essence of a negotiation process, such as: (1) at least two parties, (2) a complementary interest in an exchange, and (3) a potential opposition of interests regarding a give-and-take arrangement.

When the negotiation takes place interculturally, many factors interfere to complicate or sometimes enrich the process. Amongst many other specificities relating to the art of negotiating across cultures, we can mention that in most cases, the parties involved arrive at the table carrying with them different perceptions, cognitions, and assumptions on what is expected and on what is supposed to happen; the interests of the parties may vary in priority and in intensity, and the desired outcomes of the discussions will depend on whether these are designed for the short, medium, or long run.

As negotiating parties tend to think, feel, and behave differently when originating from diverse cultural backgrounds, misunderstandings may arise, and this happens not just at surface level (regarding protocol and body language, for example), but also at a deeper plane, as far as mutual expectations, common practices, and systems of values are concerned.

Issues that may arise when negotiators come from different cultures include, for instance[1]:

- **The type and amount of preparation invested in a negotiation**: Universalist cultures will have a tendency to have "done their homework" and will attend the negotiation meeting having prepared all the necessary documentation, drafted contracts, and developed a strategy. Particularist cultures will tend to prepare the basics, but wait until they meet the partners in person and develop a relationship before making any decisions or drafting any contracts. The "feeling" and potential prospects to be constructed will be more determinant than any piece of objective information, so not much can be prepared prior to meeting the partners. External locus of control cultures will equally prefer to leave aspects of the contract "imprecise," as a means to ensure the necessary flexibility to adapt to the particular characteristics of the business partner and also to the uncertainty of the environment. Not much can be planned in advance, so better to leave the door open. Internal locus of control cultures will prefer to maximize the chances of "winning the game" or "controlling the situation," therefore they will join the negotiation table well armed with arguments and solid analyses of potential scenarios that they will "confront" the other party with.
- **Task orientation versus interpersonal relations orientation**: Executives from "doing" cultures will "jump to the task" and maximize the number of actions done by minute. In Fons Trompenaars' terms, sequentials will try to maximize the output per unit of time invested in the task.

Therefore, the schedule of sequentials will be strictly defined and these negotiators will insist on having their timeframes respected. Synchronic negotiators, on the other hand, will want to develop the relationship first and foremost, since to them this constitutes the basis of a good deal: no good business can take place for the long run unless dealings with people are ensured and assured first. Outings, dinners, golf games, gift exchanges, endless protocol, and sightseeing are on the program for synchronics when they do business. "Dating the opponent" is done before "signing the papers" so that when the deal is closed, there will be no surprises and the future of the exchanges will be protected. These series of practices will be interpreted as a "useless waste of time" by sequentials, but in fact they are a wise investment for the future. Once you know someone, you can then concentrate on business without having to incur the transaction costs that are inevitable when your partner is a stranger.

- **General principles versus specific details**: Negotiators from individualistic, sequential, internal locus of control cultures will require specific details to be stated in the contract in order to ensure that there will be no ambiguities or misunderstandings in the future. Sometimes, people from these cultures will bring lawyers to the negotiation table to discuss matters. The main intention of people from these (generally low-context) cultures is to minimize the room for conflict in future. Negotiators from collective, synchronic, external locus of control cultures see the attempt to pre-state everything as lack of trust and lack of willingness to develop a good relationship for the long term. They would prefer (and see as a sign of goodwill) to agree on general principles and then adapt to specific situations and demands as time goes by and the relationship evolves. If the quality of the relationship is considered to be good enough, negotiators could even go beyond the agreement and deliver more than the contract demands. It is understood that in the long term, a win-win situation is to be achieved.

- In China, the now international term *guanxi* defines a series of interrelated connections of people who trust each other and who deal in business and in private under a logic of mutual favors. Within these networks, everyone knows there will always be someone to help when in distress, but there is always the pressure of loyalty to give back to those in need as well. In Japan, the term *ningsei* (in Japanese) also relates to a similar phenomenon, which carries a specific connotation of "sweet codependence," applicable in business, as much as in family relations.
- **Number of people present and the extent of their influence:** Negotiators from doing, low power distance, low uncertainty avoidance, sequential cultures would tend to delegate decision making more than others. To them, control means cost, and therefore not maximizing the use of their human resources. This explains why in general the number of people present is lower and the extent of their influence relatively high. Negotiators from high power distance, high uncertainty avoidance, synchronic cultures would tend to centralize decision-making processes and therefore the level of delegation in these cultures is lower and this may require several visits from lowly ranked people before the "big boss" arrives. Or sometimes, visiting parties are constituted by an important number of people, as those in power need to underline their status by bringing their subordinates over with him/her as advisors, trainees, secretaries, or lower management. Whereas negotiators of the previous type might sometimes consult headquarters (in particular their lawyers back home) before making a decision, they will in general have been given relatively more freedom to act and will expect action to take place quite promptly. Negotiators from the opposite type may take time discussing internally and may even wait until they go back home to make a decision or close the deal, but lawyers would not be make visible or sometimes will not even exist. The visible presence of a lawyer could at times be interpreted as failure of the relationship building and therefore the end of any further agreements.

A concrete example of differences that go beyond protocol, but have to do with below-the-surface differences in approach to negotiations due to the cross-cultural idiosyncrasies of the parties can be obtained through the analysis of the standard patterns of behavior of American negotiators when dealing with Japanese counterparts and vice-versa.

Buyer–Seller Relations in Japan and in the United States

Figure 7.1 schematizes buyer–seller relationships in the United States and in Japan when dealing intranationally and internationally.

On the right of the chart, we see the scheme of what happens when Americans buy or sell from Americans. In general, in this case, the buyer will have a relatively higher status in terms of bargaining power ("the customer is always right"), so the seller will make attempts to please his

JAPAN   USA

Buyer

Buyer

Seller

Seller

Figure 7.1. Buyer–seller relationships in Japan and in the United States.

counterpart, who in this case happens to be the money holder. Having said this, the seller will be expected to push for the interests of his or her company as much as the buyer will be expected to pull for the interests of his or hers. It will be considered as acceptable behavior that the buyer will attempt to have the shortest delivery dates, a minimum price, and payment facilities, as much as a good salesman will be expected to try to limit the benefits and conditions as much as possible without losing the sale.

In Japan, on the other hand, what is expected is a "*ningensei*" type of relationship, which means a sweet interdependence in which long-term relationships justify the sacrifice of short-term benefits. In concrete terms, in Japan, the seller will give the buyer everything he or she wants, but the buyer will not exploit this "higher status" situation, as a sign of interest in developing a longer-term relationship. In a tacit gentlemen's agreement, the buyer will not lose face by abusing his or her position of power asking for more than would be reasonable, as much as the seller will make every effort to please the customer or client.

The problem often appears then when Japanese and Americans negotiate. If an American buyer deals with a Japanese seller, the former will assume that his role is to bargain and obtain as many conditions as possible from the seller. The Japanese seller, on the other hand, will at first make enormous attempts to please the buyer, but at some point he or she will find that the expectations of the buyer are unrealistic and that the attitude of the American is pushy and disrespectful. This perception may discourage the Japanese buyer from dealing with this counterpart in the long term and therefore, the negotiation may end right there with no deal being closed.

Alternatively, when a Japanese buyer approaches an American salesperson, he will have an attitude that will certainly be less aggressive than that of the average American buyer. In fact, the Japanese buyer will be expecting the salesperson to accept the conditions without bargaining, and an attempt to alter the proposition could be perceived as a sign of disrespect and a lack of interest in developing links for the long term. The American salesperson may think he or she is doing his or her job correctly by pushing for the interests of his or her company. In fact, even when the deal may not seem the most convenient at first, if there is an interest in relationship building, in the long term the Japanese buyer will compensate those agreeing to perhaps give up some conditions for the sake of a good future business partnership.

In fact, Japanese and American businesspeople perceive both the process and the outcome of the negotiation differently. For the American negotiator, it is about a zero-sum game: whatever one wins, the other loses, just as in sports. Therefore a negotiation is understood as a business process during which each party will try to maximize profit whatever the impact on the partner may be.

The attitude described above is certainly linked to the sequential mindset of Americans, who see life as a succession of passing events, not necessarily tightly linked to each other. Today's negotiating outcome may or may not affect the future. Next time a deal needs to be made, it may or may not be with the same business partner as others in the market may be offering a more suitable product or service. Each negotiation takes place independently from those of the past and the future. The negotiators even may or may not be employed by the same organization in the future, so giving up on benefits expecting reparation in the long run would perhaps in most cases not make much sense. Besides, Americans are evaluated on performance on a short-term basis (quarterly or yearly), therefore they may be less inclined to sacrifice an immediate benefit in the hope of a larger reward later.

In most American negotiators' minds, the item that is subject to negotiation is perceived as a cake that needs to be distributed between the negotiating parties. Therefore if one party obtains a bigger share this can only happen through the detriment of the share obtained by the other counterparts. It is therefore a "win-lose game," or a "zero sum game."

The "cake" can be divided in half,

or one party can obtain 75% of the cake and the other 25% of it, or one party can obtain 60% and the other 40%... but the total sum will never exceed the total amount of the cake to be distributed, as the cake does not grow, but remains the same size no matter what is agreed. A good negotiator in the American mind, therefore, is one who does whatever may be possible to increase his or her "share of the cake," not just for his or her own personal benefit, but also for that of the company that hires him/her.

On the other hand, the Japanese mind naturally tends to understand the negotiation process as a long-term endeavor. For the Japanese buyer, as much as for the seller, developing a trusting relationship with a business partner requires effort, time, and investment. This is directly linked to their particularistic and synchronic way of thinking, according to which past, present, and future are tightly interconnected, and relationships are the main link between events happening through time and affecting profit, sustainability, and growth. Making a concession will in this context be interpreted as a sign of goodwill, attempting at developing and entertaining good quality long relationships that will generate prosperity for both sides, as opposed to an indication of weakness.

For the Japanese, the key aspect of a negotiation is relationship building, as the outcome of the particular deal is just one link of the chain of events defining a long-term pattern of mutually beneficial exchanges. Japanese buyers, as well as sellers, would attempt to make sure their counterparts are pleased after the exchange, perhaps not out of altruism, but simply because they see a potential profit for themselves in creating a win-win situation.

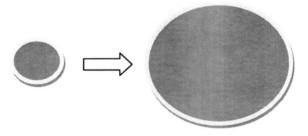

For the Japanese, therefore, the "cake" does not just get divided; it gets enlarged through relationship building, as all parties concerned will obtain more out of it either in the short or the long run. "Giving one for the team" in a collectivist culture certainly implies that the team protects each player within the big picture. That is why for the Japanese, the search for "positive sum games" and "win-win" situations is key.

The "cake" may be divided in many ways; perhaps there is one bigger portion obtained by one party in the short run, but in the long term, the cards may end up being shuffled differently and the outcome may vary.

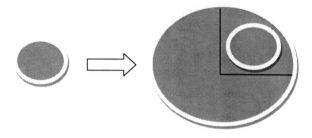

A small portion of a bigger cake may be bigger than a whole small cake; therefore enlarging the cake through relationship building becomes paramount.

Other reasons for different approaches to negotiations may be simply practical. For instance, we already discussed the case of frequency in performance evaluations in American companies, which may affect the urgency in obtaining results. A certainty of access to future cash flow is a guarantee of success for an American when facing headquarters. For Japanese businessmen, in view of their long-term orientation, what matters most is market share, particularly in family owned large firms (i.e., the car manufacturing industry). Sometimes therefore and for tangible and concrete reasons that go beyond subjective human perception and behavior, what "makes Japanese click" is not necessarily "what makes Americans click."

Just to give another example, for the Vietnamese government, which has to face high unemployment rates and sees jobs that offer low wage rates, projects that create working positions are important. For the Swiss government, which experiences low unemployment rates and high wage rates, projects that create positions are not as important, but they may be looking for something else. Therefore, whatever may be tempting for the Vietnamese may not be so for the Swiss.

Strategies for Handling Cross-Cultural Negotiations

Below is a series of examples of successful strategies that were used in cross-cultural negotiations to maximize mutual benefits with minimum cultural shock.

Example 1

An American businessman was put in charge of negotiating the sale of a significant amount of IT materials to an Egyptian group. The buyer offered to pay in trade, but the North American headquarters insisted on receiving payment in dollars. The American negotiator traveled then to Cairo, where he spent a long week socializing and discussing matters with the potential buyer. He participated in excursions, discussions, and sports; by the end of the trip he had not only signed a contract for payment in cash, but also started the development of new markets within nearby regions, thanks to the contacts established during that time.

In acting as a "particularist" and using the relationship to generate trust and mutual gain, the American businessman managed to "enlarge the cake." Time was invested in this relationship and one of the outcomes was a concession, which was not obtained out of pressure, threat, or a short-term exchange, but as an investment in the relationship which in the long term resulted into a win-win situation (and even a win-win-win one in this case).

Example 2

When American ITT and GCE of France merged in the 1980s, the French counterparts feared a "cruel, heartless, radical, and fearless takeover" and were very reluctant to cooperate and refused to trust their partners.

It was only when ITT lawyers argued that they would be following standard methodology, in full compliance with international law, which had been developed by experts and which had functioned well for a long time, that the French changed their attitude and started to collaborate rather than question.

Taking advantage of the high uncertainty avoidance of the French, the skillful Americans assumed all responsibility regarding the process, which sounded both rational and already tested. When facing what within a Cartesian logic seemed to be a methodology that not only discharged them from the risk involved in such big undertakings, but also seemed logical, well structured, and proved, the French happily—or unhappily—gave in to an operating mode that would easily point the blame away them in case of failure. The Americans, then, had "*carte blanche*" to go ahead and implement their ways. The success in this negotiation for the Americans was based on (1) convincing the French that there was rationality behind their operations and not just trial and error, and (2) assuming responsibility in the process, liberating their partners from the risk of blame in case the whole enterprise failed.

Examples 3 and 4

When this American multinational wanted to develop trade with China in the business of soft drinks in the 1970s, the first thing they did was to send their most promising chemical engineers for training in Chinese culture, language, literature, music, and history for a year. This was the key differentiating factor that allowed them not only to enter this huge market, but also to lead it.

When former President of South Africa Nelson Mandela was in prison, he spent most of his time studying the language, literature, and all forms of art expression developed by the subculture that had put him in jail and kept him in there for many years. Once free, he explained to the world that it was only through the deep understanding of the ways of thinking and feeling of all South Africans that he could one day reunite his country and lead it towards equality, freedom, unity, and fraternity.

The same way that "*ningensei*" needs to be more than learned, probably even incepted in order to be successful in dealing with the Japanese, sharing the Chinese sensitivity to interpersonal dealings is key to ensuring a long-term fruitful relationship. It is possible to arrive there naturally and simply. Often this requires effort, as intuition plays a great role in understanding and meta-communicating with others, in particular when they originate from different parts of the world.

Example 5

During negotiations regarding the development and launch of the Channel Tunnel, British and French parties agreed to act and behave local whenever the meetings took place in each nation.

This very specific agreement entails the very British sense of politeness with the very French sense of justice. It is an extremely interesting example of a give-give situation in which two of the greatest empires of the world make an effort to show that they are not attempting to overcome the other nation, but to conclude an international agreement by accepting that the tunnel will be neither French nor English and that therefore there will be no imposition of practices or any threats to established idiosyncrasies. These mutual concessions were proof of goodwill and of the shared impression that goodwill was necessary for the successful conclusion of this important deal.

The Employee/Employer Relationship in Different Countries[2]

Just as we observed how aspects of national culture can clearly affect corporate culture in terms of Hofstede's and d'Iribarne's observations, we can explore in what ways national culture affects intercultural business negotiations within the workplace, in particular in case of international transfers, working with expatriate employees, and other employer/employee situations. A few examples are noted below.

In the **United States**, the work relationship is considered a mutually beneficial commercial agreement. The employee exchanges time, effort, knowledge, and capacity for employment conditions including salary, career prospects, reputation, benefits, and so forth. This relationship is mostly materialistic and defined and ruled by law. Both the employee and the employer consider their links as professional and would find it natural if either of the parties decide one day to end the contract, as long as the contractual conditions for termination are respected until the end. In this sense, employee and employer, in spite of hierarchical differences (also established and limited by the contract), are basically equal parties trading within the job market. Demand and supply would determine who has more power at each stage of the process.

In **Japan and Korea**, the employee/employer relationship has a "family" connotation. Even if there is a contract of employment, the relationship is based on a tacit psychological contract with its strongest components being mutual trust and loyalty. The employee will do everything the employer wants, but the employer will not abuse the employee. The employee accepts tacitly that the employer knows more about what is best for the company that is ensuring his survival and that of his family, and he also knows that the employer cares for his own well-being. The employer could be described by a Westerner as a "benevolent autocrat" as his decisions will be accepted by the employee without major arguments. The employer, on the other hand, would not abuse the employee, as that would damage his own image. The employer is supposed to have a duty of decency that needs to be shown by not abusing his power.

In **France**, the relationship is based on honor and respect for authority. Employers in France know that the most fearful event they would have to face is general grievance, as this is the only movement they cannot control. Tribunals also tend to act rather quickly and to favor employees, so "Proud'hommes" (Employment Tribunal) appears as a fearful word to the ears of a French employer. Moreover, being unemployed is not generally perceived as a shameful state, but as the result of unfair treatment from the upper classes. Therefore there is no great social prejudice preventing employees from setting themselves into the very generous benefits system when and if required.

Apart from that eventuality, employees function under the apathy–rebellion logic. Their opinions are not heard, communication takes place on a top-down, unilateral basis, and a system of filters that prevent feedback from employees to the top is installed. Those filters are in general middle managers who tacitly assume the duty of preventing top managers from being disturbed by daily matters regarding employee's needs, requests, and demands. In general, employees accept the situation for as long as they enjoy part of the honorable benefits that top managers consent to provide them with and most of the time they develop an apathetic attitude towards what happens, accepting their own fate of submission without even questioning it. As members of a classist society, the French would naturally tolerate the fact that there is a ruling group that at the same time makes the rules and pushes for their compliance on one side and another group that simply complies in exchange for protection. A shared sense of honor amongst the higher class prevents most managers from abuse, and when it happens unions intervene. In general, unions act to preserve the integrity of the lower strata of society, but they hardly ever consider it necessary to help them face managers in a *"mano a mano"* (face-to-face) confrontation. At best, unions would just take employees back to a tolerable state of circumstances, but never to a place in which they would actually have enough bargaining power to seriously negotiate with the higher class.

In terms of power, the French scheme would be difficult to draw, as the distance of power and logic of honor would well resemble the Japanese buyer-seller status structure. Indeed, the French employer would in this comparative metaphor be the "buyer of workforce," who does not expect the seller to bargain on his offer, and the employee playing the "seller of work power" who accepts the lenient conditions of the buyer of his workforce without arguing. Within this logic of honor and hierarchical respect, the international customer of goods produced by the company would be an outsider who should respect the honor of the employee by not disturbing him or her with foreign practices to be adapted to (being a worker provides dignifying status that needs to be respected), and even if the seller should accommodate in principle to please the potential client, he will not do so if this means potential trouble with unions or generalized dissatisfaction in-house, as one of the duties of the buyer of workforce services is to protect people who work for him or her.

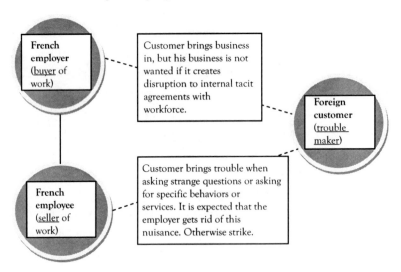

The foreign customer may bring money in for the short term, but if this means that with his habits and expectations the (always in tension) relationship between employers and employees may be disrupted, then in the long term harmony may be threatened and this would lead to chaos. Therefore, the foreign habits that could be annoying to employees should be avoided even at the expense of losing a short-term deal (the French are particularist and synchronic after all!).

This may explain at least partially why the French are so bad at customer service. They do not see the customer as the one who brings the money that will pay his salary, but as a potential disturbance that employers ought to protect them from as part of the honorable tacit agreement between them.

In **the Netherlands**, where equality determines and rules over most relationships, employers and employees operate and deal with little hierarchical boundaries. Decisions need to be validated and backed up by consensus and in general discussions are not controversial, but aiming at pursuing the common good. Fairness is a key word and transactions may take time, as consensus needs to be reached and shared by all parties concerned. And all parties are concerned!

Using This Information

Negotiations are behavioral processes that are complicated in nature. When the intercultural aspect enters into play, more complications arise and deals get more difficult to close.

It is easy to fall into the trap of searching for tips that would render the exercise more bearable or easy to close. But it would be advisable to remember that when negotiating internationally, still waters run deep and worse than not knowing how to behave when confronting diverse parties in business is to think one masters their behaviors when one does not. This is probably not just the best way to render oneself ridiculous, but overall it is the surest way to lead any project into failure.

Exercises

1. Based on the reading above, list and explain why and how different frameworks for analysis (masculinity/femininity, uncertainty avoidance, etc.) affect behavior in the cultures described.

_____

_____

_____

_____

_____
_____
_____
_____
_____
_____
_____
_____
_____
_____
_____
_____
_____
_____
_____
_____
_____
_____
_____
_____

2. Imagine how negotiations between employers and employees (salaries, promotions, bargaining through unions…) can take place in the different cultures described. How could conflict situations be handled between and inside these cultures?

_____
_____
_____
_____
_____
_____
_____
_____
_____
_____

CHAPTER 8

Cross-Cultural Conflict and Conflict Resolution

Contextualizing Background Information

Hellriegel, Slocum, and Woodman[1] have defined "conflict" as follows: "Any situation in which there are incompatible goals, cognitions, or emotions within or between individuals or groups that lead to opposition." This definition allows the anticipation of a few potential areas of complexity that would certainly become more acute when conflict takes an intercultural dimension.

Incompatible *goals* can certainly cause disruption within a business setting, but when people involved in the conflict are from different cultural backgrounds, such disruption can rapidly escalate. Reasons for greater confusion can include the fact that it may become more difficult to make goals compatible, but also because the ranking of the goals may be different and so could the notion of goals themselves.

For instance, whereas the main goal of a series of meetings could be in the mind of a Chinese negotiator the setup of an appropriate arena of interactions that would ensure proper exchanges for the future, the aim of the same negotiation for an American counterpart could be the closing of a unique deal. The difference between a synchronic and a sequential culture in this case becomes rather important and obvious, and it could lead to misunderstandings, frustrations, arguments, and the end of a potentially profitable business deal. In this case, it could happen that even if the American negotiator states the objectives clearly and makes numerous attempts at underlining his position with clarity, still the Chinese partner would not pay attention to them; in fact, he or she would actually assume the Americans ought not to rush into agreements without a complete overview of the background conditions. Any other sort of behavior would be considered unwise.

Differences in *cognitions* could certainly present challenges as well and at many levels. Executives from high power distance cultures would prefer not to delegate much to their subordinates, so when dealing with partners of the same hierarchical level from low power distance cultures, the amount of information they would have in hand or even have access to would be much more limited. Besides, if the former negotiators are from a high uncertainty avoidance culture, then they would also deny their ignorance on certain specific aspects, which would make matters much worse.

In terms of differences in *emotions*, businesspeople from emotional cultures would have a tendency to express their feelings very openly, which could distract partners from neutral cultures, puzzling them, irritating them, or even making them misunderstand what the real issues are. Neutrals could seem rather cold to emotional business partners and their distance could be interpreted as lack of interest, nonappreciation of the concessions made or dislike of what is being offered, including the warm hospitality that emotional people usually offer to foreigners they deal professionally with.

If besides being emotional, the business partners in question are also diffuse, then an attempt at separating business from private feelings of friendship or loyalty could seriously vex them. And if on top of being emotional and diffuse, the businesspeople in question are also from high context cultures, it would then probably become very difficult to understand why they react in a very angry manner when there are attempts to "get to the nitty-gritty."

Situations of conflict that may arise when individuals involved come from different cultures (again according to Hellriegel et al.) include:

- **Goal conflict**: a situation in which desired end states or preferred outcomes appear to be incompatible.
- **Cognitive conflict**: a situation in which ideas or thoughts are perceived as incompatible.
- **Affective conflict**: a situation in which feelings or emotions are incompatible. That is, people literally become angry with one another.

Below are some examples of cultural misunderstanding that could easily lead to conflict because of differences in thinking, feeling, and expressing ideas in different cultures. The following passages illustrate some of the potential areas of misunderstanding:

Passage I

PETE: Did you talk to the accreditation body from the UK? How did it go?

THERESA: Yes, sure I had to. But it went really well. What a bunch of gentlemen! So polite and sophisticated!

PETE: Did you really tell them that we would not be able to deliver all the figures they are asking for by the end of the week?

THERESA: Of course, I told him that we just did not have all the materials in hand and that some of the issues were just too complex for us to deal with.

PETE: So?

THERESA: He just said, "Oh, that is quite inconvenient, really" and changed the subject.

PETE: Great! Everything is OK then. Oufff!

In the above dialog we see a clear example of upcoming **cognitive** conflict, derived from a very different approach in communications. The American partners misunderstood their English counterpart, to whom the expression "that's a bit of a nuisance" means in fact that there will be great problems caused by the forthcoming delays. After the conversation with the accreditation body, the Americans probably felt over-relaxed and will probably not make too many efforts to redress the situation immediately. On the other hand, the English will probably react quite strongly, perhaps even denying the accreditation stamp, as to their knowledge they have very clearly stated that it was not OK not to present the figures. When the Americans realize they will not have been accredited, they will be very angry with the British for not letting them know in advance that there would be penalties. The English will probably refer to the contract and avoid any sort of confrontation, while having their rights reinforced.

Passage II

MS THOMPSON: Are you having any sort of personal problems, Xiao Yu? I could not help but noticing that you have been sick a lot since we nominated you Head of Department. Are you all right? Is there anything we can do for you?

XIAO YU: I'm sorry, ma'am.

MS THOMPSON: Are you doing OK? Are there any aspects of the job that we could help you with, perhaps?

XIAO YU: I would not want to be a nuisance. Thank you very much for noticing I was not feeling that well.

MS THOMPSON: You have so much potential and you are so good at what you do. Far much more suited for the task than Mr. Wei or Mr. Jiao, I would have thought....

XIAO YU: Oh, no, ma'am. They are very good, and they have been here much longer than I.

There is in this passage a clear case of goal conflict. In China, typically an ascribed country, progress and success are not measured by achievements, but through loyalty, respect for the hierarchy, and seniority. Xiao Yu sincerely must have felt in a bad position when promoted over her older colleagues, because she was put in a position in which she looks like someone who did not respect her colleagues, but who betrayed them. In a corner between doing her best at her job and losing the appreciation of her peers, Xiao Yucan only escape by faking sickness, but still, she would have preferred that her American boss had promoted one of the other employees.

In China, the objective of a career is to achieve recognition through loyalty and respect of the elderly. In America, it is to do so through performance and hard work. There is certainly a tacit conflict in this case between the American system and the Chinese one, which manifests through the loss of valuable potential hours of work and a bad office atmosphere. If on top of everything it is a young lady causing disruption, then this can be considered as a very serious affront.

Passage III

BJORN: Hola, Pablo, how is it going?

PABLO: Very well, Sir. I was just reviewing the theory of the hierarchy of needs by Maslow with this student here.

BJORN: I know, please remember I used to teach Human Resources Management before I was Dean. Actually, I overheard you; what you were telling the student isn't exactly right.

PABLO: No?

BJORN: No. The security needs go below the needs for affection according to this theory. Look at the chart here, see? First basic needs, then safety needs, then...

PABLO: Thank you, sir.

Pablo has certainly felt devastated after his boss embarrassed him publicly in front of the student. Pablo is probably from a diffuse, high power distance, high uncertainty avoidance culture, and having a boss tell him how to do things is an open affront.

Pablo may have not reacted immediately, but he is certainly hurt and humiliated. He feels he is not being considered by his superior and he has lost authority over someone to whom he ought to have been seen as a role model. The long-term consequences of such an episode could escalate if this sort of scene is repeated: the employee may resign, or he may contribute to boycotting the boss, or he may find the way to embarrass the dean in another manner. But nothing very positive will come out of this interaction.

Having said this, Bjorn's intentions were certainly good and honorable. He must have thought that his way of acting was generous and understanding. He is for sure from a low power distance culture (probably Scandinavian?) and to him, what matters is that the job gets done. Bjorn may even have thought of himself as a generous and understanding open-minded boss, who respects his employee's rank because he asked Pablo to go to him in case there was a problem.

Solving Conflict Situations in the Workplace

In order to resolve conflict situations, structural methods of conflict management can help. Here are some examples:

- **Dominance through position**: Two persons or two groups are in conflict. They call a third party to make a decision that the two others will accept and respect. For example, if two CEOs of different subsidiaries in different countries disagree on a course of action to undertake, a CEO from headquarters or from a third independent subsidiary may be called upon to make a decision that the other two parties will have to respect.
- **Decoupling**: Avoid having people work together if they do not get along.
- **Linking pins**: Find people who facilitate dialog between two conflicting parties. They should be intermediaries accepted by both sides. For example, a bi-national person could help two people from two different cultures to understand each other.

Dominance through position works best in universalist cultures, because it looks like a democratic decision. In particularist cultures, on the other hand, this system would tempt the conflicting parties to try to hold the attention and benefits from the decision maker in order to apply them for their own profit.

Decoupling would probably work in diffuse cultures, and especially in high context ones, where harmony is key. As conflict in these cultures is often perceived as the major source of energy waste and profitability drain, avoiding having the parties involved meet may seem as a very reasonable choice in order to ensure harmony. In achievement cultures, such a procedure would be seen as childish and unprofessional. Workers are supposed to leave their emotions aside (in particular in neutral cultures) and concentrate in working, no matter what their issues with other colleagues could be.

Linking pins is a very commonly used technique, but more often than not it is already too late in the conflict when parties call for it. If a conflict has already been pronounced, having someone intervene can cause disruption, rather than facilitate mutual understanding. It needs therefore to be avoided in these cases. Having said this, in times when negotiations need to take place or when international parties feel they may need assistance before the conflict has gone too deep, linking pins can be very useful, in particular to reduce anxiety and have participants release tension and feel more at ease. With a lighter heart, it is often much simpler to carry on with a negotiation or to take a common action together.

The Gladwin and Walter[2] Model of Cross-Cultural Conflict

The Basic Model and the Situations

Gladwin and Walter produced a model based on the importance given to self-interest vis-à-vis the priority given to the relationship maintenance. The crossing of these two dimensions gives place to four basic attitudes towards conflict situations, which are more or less likely to appear in different cultures. The four possible options are: compete, collaborate, avoid, and accommodate (Figure 8.1).

In "compete" situations, each one of the parties involved in conflict will try to maximize the outcomes of the dispute to their own, immediate benefit. The relationship with the other side will be only limited to the one specific transaction or situation, and therefore the shared aim will be just to take as much as possible from the other for one's own benefit at the particular point in time.

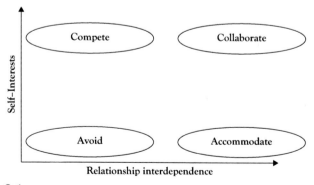

Figure 8.1.

In "collaborate" situations, not only the interests of each party should be maximized, but also the relationship should be kept. Obtaining everything one party wants at one time at the expense of the other could limit potential future collaboration, therefore none of the aspects should be looked down upon.

In "avoid" situations, neither is the expected outcome worth a fight nor is the relationship worth keeping, therefore, both sides will stop the contact and with it the opportunities for opposition.

In "accommodate" situations, conflict will be eliminated through the giving away of all interests by one side for the sake of the other one involved. The main outcome of the conflict in this case, would be the maintenance of the business relationship exclusively.

The first of the four combinations, in which both self-interest and relationship interdependence are to be protected, is called "**collaborate**" (Figure 8.2). This option is favored by feminine cultures, which understand the need to push for achievement and progress, while they see an interest in having everyone remain happy with the outcome. For instance, in typically feminine cultures such as Sweden or Holland, disputes between management and unions often are solved after long discussions in which the interests of all parties concerned are taken into consideration.

"Collaborate" is often used as a preferred option in particularist cultures, as it is usually expected to come across situations in which the benefits of developing a lasting business relationship may exceed those of one particularly positive, but immediate business outcome. Giving favors in

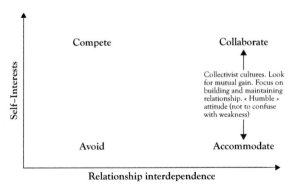

Figure 8.2.

the present may have more important repercussions in the future, and these may compensate for an immediate small loss.

In some collectivist cultures, like in Japan, making concessions can represent a way to show goodwill in business and to expose intentions to develop a lasting and profitable relationship. This can often be perceived as weakness, but in most cases it is not the case. Giving today may just be a very polite way to signal that favors may be expected from the other side in the future.

The second of the combinations is **"compete"** (Figure 8.3). In this option, the contenders find themselves within win-lose situations, where whatever one does not take, the other will. Negotiators from sequential, achieving, individualistic societies are usually presented as good examples of this type of conflict management, as they do not see the point in continuing the relationship further, in particular when they need to show concrete results back home at headquarters, as they will be evaluated upon them. In "compete" situations there is always a "winner" and a "loser," therefore it is understandable that each party will push to be on the winning side. The "pie," or totality of assets on stake, cannot be reduced or enlarged through discussions, promises, or by "sending the elevator back," and therefore whatever is at stake needs to be divided and it will be those who push harder that will get the most out of the exchange. It is a zero-sum game, because whatever one party will take, the other will lose.

The third combination available is **"avoid"** (Figure 8.4). This option is preferred by high context cultures, particularists, diffuses, and high power distance cultures because it allows to keep harmony. Particularists may

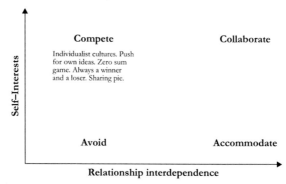

Figure 8.3.

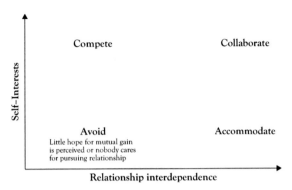

Figure 8.4.

decide that they are not interested in keeping the relationship alive with this partner and will avoid the conflict by stopping their dealings with him. But if they are not sure there will never be another chance for positive exchanges with them, they may chose not to openly express anger or negative feelings, but to "get away from the table" instead.

Similarly, people from diffuse cultures may estimate that this partner is not interesting or this particular deal is not worth entering into a conflict, but that having a bad rapport with the counterpart could damage their network, so they would rather not complicate the situation and go ahead just ignoring the facts and walking away.

In high power distant cultures, keeping a good relationship with the authorities may sound like utopia to most lower ranked employees. Besides, their chances of obtaining anything out of the powerful could seem impossible. Therefore, even if the self-interest is not fulfilled, many people in such a situation would deem it irrelevant to enter a discussion and would go on working apathetically, doing the minimum not to enter a conflict situation, but nothing more than that.

In the "**accommodate**" option one of the parties declines the totality of its interests on the matter, for the privilege of the other side exclusively (Figure 8.5). This type of behavior usually happens when there is acknowledgment and acceptance of the superiority of one side over the other (for example in the case of the buyer/seller relationship in Japan, as explained in chapter 7), typically in high power distance cultures or in high uncertainty avoidance ones, in which the fear of the outcome of the conflict could overcome the necessity to preserve one's self-interest.

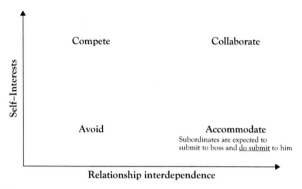

Figure 8.5.

This behavior could also occur in particularistic cultures, in which a personal sense of loyalty may have developed. The sentiment of "honorable debt" vis-à-vis a partner could justify the giving away of certain rights or of certain privileges, goods, or conditions for the mere sake of pride. In many countries, the sense of honor, linked to "cleansing one's name" or saving one's reputation can go a long way in terms of surrendering own interests for the benefit of one cause.

Conflict Resolution and Intercultural Attitudes

When two parties confront each other from different perspectives, attempting conflict resolution from different angles, the general situation can quickly become more complicated, generating upsetting dynamics of false expectations, delusion, and disappointment.

Figures 8.6–8.11 represent potential misunderstandings deriving from the attitudes originating from diverse mental programmings and how these are received by intercultural interlocutors.

Case I: The Compete–Accommodate Misunderstanding

When one of the parties comes to the conflict mediation table with a "compete" attitude and faces an "accommodate" one, then the former will obtain everything from the latter at his expense. The "accommodating" party will just give away for a while and then probably stop dealing with the other when the cost will surpass by far the value of the relationship.

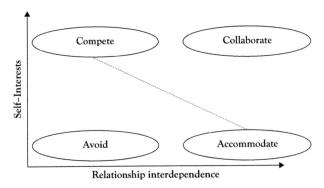

Figure 8.6.

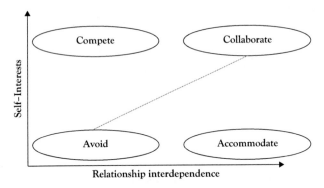

Figure 8.7.

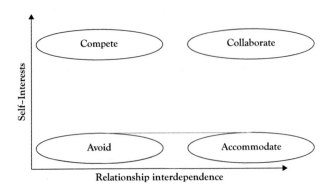

Figure 8.8.

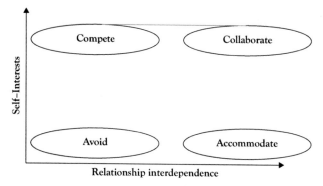

Figure 8.9.

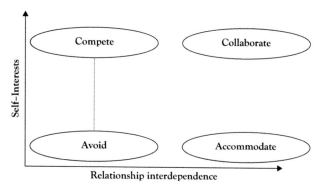

Figure 8.10.

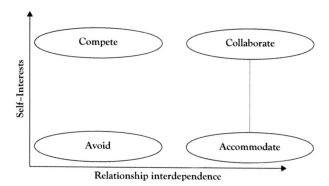

Figure 8.11.

This is the typical case of the buyer–seller relationship we examined in the chapter about negotiations. The American salesperson would do his/her best to please the buyer, but the latter would ask for the moon. In France, when managers push too hard on employees, the reaction manifests through strikes and breaking of goods, even through kidnappings, but most of the time, they obey their boss without questioning his demands and requests.

Case II: The Collaborate–Avoid Misunderstanding

When one party comes to the negotiation table aiming at collaborating, but the other is just willing to avoid, the conflict can end up in different ways. One of them is that the collaborating part will get tired of trying and eventually give up on making efforts to please the counterpart. The other is that the avoiding part will take as much as is offered without giving much away, which in the medium to long run will upset the collaborating partner. In some cases, the conflict is solved by the change of attitude of the avoiding part, which at some stage may see a benefit in collaborating and give up apathy. This kind of relationship is being perceived sometimes between unions from feminine cultures who attempt at participating in decisions being made by companies with headquarters in high power distance countries. For instance, if a French company was to operate in Finland, the Finnish unions would attempt at collaborating with management, but their ideas would probably be ignored unless they make use of force at some point.

Case III: The Avoid–Accommodate Misunderstanding

When one party wants to avoid and the other is in an "accommodate" mood, the consequences are similar to the ones explained above, but to a greater extent. The interest in the relationship may be even greater for the accommodate part than was for the collaborate one because the latter has also self-interest at stake.

The case of sweatshops in India could be an example of avoid–accommodate relationship in which the boss has no interest in listening to the needs of the workers, who have no choice but to subscribe to what is imposed to them as their only means of subsistence.

Case IV: The Compete–Collaborate Misunderstanding

When one of the parties is interested in the relationship or in doing business in the future and the other is not, then the collaborative side may find it very annoying having to deal with such a partner. At first, the collaborative side may make concessions, but at some point, and because there will be no similar response from the other side, the concessions will soon end and the deal will turn into a competition, but the collaborative side will seriously start looking for alternative parties to deal with in the future and only go back to the same partner if there are no reasonable alternatives in hand.

Case V: The Compete–Avoid Misunderstanding

In cases where the compete attitude meets an avoidance one, there is rarely conflict unless the conflicting party finds a way to irritate the avoider to a point in which there is no other alternative, but to enter a dispute. When such is the case, the avoiding side will respond rather violently and attempt to end the argument as soon as possible and in a dramatic manner. In French companies, this is what often happens when an employee dares contradict a manager: at first the manager will ignore him, but after a few confrontations, and if the union does not mediate, the manager will just call for a financial arrangement or go for a lawsuit.

Case VI: The Collaborate–Accommodate Misunderstanding

When one party wants to accommodate and the other wants to collaborate, conflict will probably not last for long. It will probably be up to the collaborating side to set the rules of the game and for the accommodating side to accept them. This is the case of negotiations between Scandinavians and Japanese, where conflict often arises on communication styles rather than in content (high versus low context).

Exercise

Now discuss with colleagues and find concrete examples of cross-cultural conflict situations that you have experienced or that you have heard of and comment on them in the light of the previous exercises.

CHAPTER 9

Diversity Management

Other Forms of Diversity and Subcultures

Sophie Hennekam

In chapter 5 we discussed the development and functioning of a particular subculture, namely corporate culture, in which values (or at least practices) were shared by people composing them.

In this chapter we will explore the impact of other subcultures and their insertion into companies. Diversity, when appropriately managed, can easily translate into profit maximization, greater production, and overall satisfaction. Needless to say, it is the greatest generator of creativity. On the other hand, when a company does not profit from this asset, it immediately becomes a liability, creating cost, loss of opportunities, and sometimes even very expensive and complicated lawsuits.

An Introduction to Diversity Management

As a result of demographic changes like immigration, the steady rise in women's labor participation, and the aging population, the workplace is getting increasingly diverse. These changes require managers able to deal with employees who differ from one another in terms of gender, culture, ethnicity, age, sexuality, and physical ability. Over the past decades different approaches have been used to deal with these differences. These different approaches will be outlined briefly below.

Approaches to Diversity: From Assimilation to Pluralism

In the past, the diverse backgrounds, experiences, skills, values, norms, and behaviors of employees were not valued. Organizations even tried to eliminate the differences between employees, a process called assimilation. New employees of an organization were socialized in such a way that they would reject their own norms, values, beliefs, and practices and embrace those of the organization. Organizations that value assimilation over diversity emphasize the need to create a homogeneous organization instead of capitalizing on the differences that make their employees unique and valuable. This is called the melting pot approach.

The other approach is called the salad bowl approach and refers to the concept of pluralism. Pluralism and assimilation are each other's opposite on the acculturation continuum. Pluralism is the acculturation process by which employees assimilate a limited number of norms, values, beliefs, and practices while preserving important aspects of their identity. Here, individuals are encouraged to bring their unique background, experiences, and personality to the workplace. This approach is called the salad bowl approach because we can still "see" the different parts of which the salad was made, while the different "ingredients" of the melting pot have become invisible.

Approaches to Diversity: From Affirmative Action to Inclusion

Although the need for a diverse workforce has been acknowledged for quite a while, the reasons behind the diversity efforts have changed. With the arrival of antidiscrimination laws organizations had to find ways to comply with the legal requirements. Diversity management was nothing more than a legally defensive position. An organization with a diverse workforce could argue that they were not guilty of discrimination based on their workforce demographics representing the demographics of the local community. This is called affirmative action (AA) or representational diversity, where different minority groups are "represented" in the organization by meeting the quotas for the employment of different minorities. Although this does increase diversity at the workplace, it does not necessarily mean that the employees that belong to a minority feel included and appreciated or occupy positions at the same hierarchical level as employees that do not belong to minority groups. In other words, diversity was not managed properly. Managers had to learn how to communicate effectively with individuals from diverse backgrounds, mentor and guide them, and create an organizational culture of inclusion where all employees feel valued in order to be able to reap the benefits of a diverse workforce. A need for an inclusive culture emerged.

Visible or Invisible: Representational Versus Behavioral Diversity

Definitions of diversity tend to be very restricted to visible features and characteristics of individuals, concealing the intense diversity that less obvious individual differences can bring to the workplace. A broader and more complex definition of diversity does not just incorporate such characteristics as gender, skin color, physical ability, socioeconomic background, age, or sexual orientation. There are other, usually less immediately obvious characteristics held by individuals at work that make workplaces rich with diversity and difference.

It was argued that representational diversity would not lead to the suggested benefits of diversity since having a certain percentage of women, Jews, or employees over the age of 50 does not imply that these employees differ from one another in behavioral aspects. Relying on the visible aspects is nowadays increasingly seen as inappropriate to enhance diversity.

Organizations are starting to recognize that behavioral diversity, as the opposite of representational diversity, is the type of diversity they are looking for. Behavioral diversity does not look at the visible aspects of their employees, but wants employees who differ from one another in terms of personality, ways of dealing with conflict and decision making, ways of communicating, methods of learning, levels of motivation or stress, and task related ideas or inputs. All of these differences may be either unrelated, or only loosely linked to the more conventional indicators of diversity. Behavioral diversity is therefore increasingly being advocated by organizations that wish to benefit from a truly diverse workforce.

Advantages of Diversity

Over the past few years, the issue of diversity management has attracted a great deal of business and academic interest. Business academics and practitioners alike have argued that promoting diversity in the workplace can be a source of sustainable competitive advantage. A sustainable competitive advantage should be valuable, rare, imperfectly imitable, and non-substitutable. Human and organizational capitals especially, such as an organizational culture, are difficult to imitate and therefore most suitable to obtain a sustainable competitive advantage. Experts contend that organizations can leverage real business benefits if they recognize, celebrate, and build on their employees' differences in gender, race, sexual orientation, religion, age, personality, and other demographic or psychosocial factors.

One advantage of an organization with a diverse workforce is that it can attract top quality talent from increasingly diverse labor pools. It is suggested that the best people from all demographic and cultural groups will be attracted to those organizations that appreciate the value they bring to the workplace. For example, the Dutch bank Rabobank has implemented several policies on diversity with the result that it has successfully increased its talent pool.

Once recruited, these diverse employees bring a number of benefits to the company. They have the ability to relate more effectively and sell to markets that are themselves multicultural and diverse. Armed with a diverse pool of employers, it is argued, companies can have access to better information on how to reach previously untapped markets. The diversity efforts of IBM are a case in point. By recruiting a more diverse workforce, the company was able to tap the knowledge of its minority employees and target new, profitable markets.

A diverse workforce can solve problems more creatively, innovate more powerfully, and can generally enhance their corporate image and reputation. The diversity policy pursued by Randstad, a recruitment consultancy, has contributed to a high percentage of employee satisfaction (98%), and to high numbers of temporary workers who would recommend Randstad (97%). The competitive advantage of this level of satisfaction, and thus the enhancement of their reputation, is clearly visible in the company's continuous growth in market share.

Barriers to the Implementation of a Diversity-Friendly Policy

In Europe, the implementation of policies and practices that can enhance diversity is often a problem since there exist considerable hurdles to the effective implementation of the business case for diversity. As reported in successive surveys conducted by the European Business Test Panel, the introduction in European companies of equality and diversity policies has been inhibited by organizational barriers, including confusing strategies, a lack of time and financial resources, and an absence of strategic guidance.

Other researchers find that, in Europe, the proliferation of diversity management practices is being impeded by a lack of managerial support, failure to empower employees and include them in decision-making processes, differing expectations, stereotyping, lack of mentoring and access to formal and informal networks, isolation and soloing, and tokenism. Traditional human resource management systems constitute another barrier to diversity because in many cases, the organization's historical methods of recruiting, motivating, and retaining workers are more conducive to homogeneity.

Organizational culture can also form a barrier. A strong organizational culture in itself is not necessarily good or bad for diversity. However, some cultures may constitute a barrier to diversity because of the content of their core values. If at its core, the organization has a strong culture that values competitiveness, aggressiveness, dominance, and interprets supportiveness or gentleness as weakness, many employees from minority groups may experience the organization as intimidating and unwelcoming.

But organizational barriers are not the only type of barriers. Psychological or human barriers can also play an important role. The preference for similar others is a human barrier to diversity. In this regard, research has shown that culturally and demographically homogeneous groups develop good working relationships more quickly than heterogeneous groups, with the result that homogeneous groups reach performance targets earlier than heterogeneous groups do.

A second human barrier to diversity is the impact of social identity. Social identity theory assumes that the status relations between social groups are often unequal, and that social groups are in competition with each other for status and power. Individuals have multiple selves or identities dependent on the context and this identification as a member of a certain social group influences their behavior or attitudes. Turner's social identity theory is linked to the theory of self-categorization since individuals develop a social identity through the process of self-categorization. Through self-categorization and group membership, individuals develop a social identity, which serves as a social-cognitive schema for their group-related behavior. Choosing a certain social identity also has consequences such as stereotyping, prejudice, discrimination, and conflict. Discrimination towards members of socially devalued groups by members of high-status social groups can be considered a form of social rejection. Experiencing social rejection in the form of perceived discrimination may deprive individuals of their need to belong and negatively influences in-group evaluations, both of which can have negative psychological consequences. Social identities are so important to people that they will work to enhance the status of the social groups to which they belong in order to maintain a positive self-image. Members of high-status groups are considerably more likely to discriminate against low-status out-groups than the reverse, and members of low-status groups will often discriminate in favor of the high-status out-group.

Social identity groups also develop images or stereotypes of each other. Stereotypes of low-status groups are often negative. Stereotypes are activated automatically and unconsciously when people come into contact with members of other social groups. People have an automatic negative reaction to low-status group members. Even people with the best intentions are influenced by the automatic activation of unconsciously held negative stereotypes about low-status groups. The automatic activation of stereotypes can pose a barrier to the recognition of people's qualifications and achievements.

Linked to the above mentioned barrier of stereotypes is the problem of discrimination, the different treatment of individuals or groups based on arbitrary ascriptive or acquired criteria such as sex, race, religion, age, marital or parental status, disability, sexual orientation, political opinions, socioeconomic background, and trade union membership and activities.

Methods That Facilitate Integration

Although an increasing number of organizations acknowledge the benefits of a diverse workforce, there are also many barriers to overcome.

Several methods can be used to facilitate the integration of minorities at the workplace.

One facility organizations can offer is support policies. In order to facilitate the achievement and performance of certain minority groups, organizations need to acknowledge and adjust to the additional challenges that may be relevant to certain specific dimensions of diversity. Women, racial minorities, people with disabilities, older employees, and so on may face difficulties that are not faced by other members of the organization.

Secondly, organizations have to recognize that their employees live different lives. Lifestyle diversity is of increasing importance, since society knows an increasing number of mono-parent families or dual-earning families and more and more employees express the need for a better work-life balance. Childcare resources, flexible working arrangements, buildings designed for people with disabilities, and so forth will have to be made available.

Furthermore, stereotypes and other barriers can obstruct the participation or performance of minority employees. The development of networks, mentors, and role models for diverse group members is an important dimension of organizational development initiatives designed to support and manage diversity.

Diversity training can also help the effective integration of minority groups in an organization. This type of training should start by increasing the awareness of the different challenges faced by different employees within the organization and the stereotypical attitudes employees have about the different groups in their organization. After the awareness-based part of the training, a competence and skills based training is necessary in order to work successfully together. Employees should keep their unique characteristics while avoiding damaging processes such as dysfunctional interpersonal conflict, miscommunication, higher levels of stress, slower decision making, and problems with group cohesiveness.

Women in International Business

The participation of women in the workforce is increasing. However, women do face different challenges than their male colleagues at work. The glass ceiling, stereotypes, career interruptions, and their leadership style will be discussed.

Glass Ceiling

The glass ceiling refers to the invisible barrier that keeps women and minorities from rising above a certain level in corporations. Beliefs and attitudes held by organizational members, as well as contextual aspects of the organization contribute to the barriers that impede women's career advancement. The following barriers can be identified: perceptions and stereotyping, corporate climate, and corporate practices.

Many negative perceptions and stereotypes about women exist. These can lead to a self-fulfilling prophecy where women start behaving in accordance with these stereotypes. The lack of role models forms a related barrier to career advancement.

The corporate climate is often hostile, or at least unreceptive, towards diversity. In most organizations that are male-led, the good old-boy network still exists, and women have been largely excluded from these networks. The benefits of informal networking are well acknowledged as important to upward mobility, including information exchange, career planning, professional support, and increased visibility. Also, care responsibilities make it difficult for women to be present at important occasions.

Corporate practices form another barrier for women, since women get assigned those positions considered suitable for women, decreasing their chances of promotion and career advancement. The lack of mentors here is an important barrier, since mentoring is an important factor of a successful career.

There are some initiatives that organizations can take to reduce or remove these barriers. First of all, a change in organizational culture and corporate practices is needed if an organization wants to keep talented women. Readdressing human resources policies and practices and changing the organizational culture and executive attitudes should help organizations retain highly talented women. Policies that support the promotion of qualified women to management positions are also needed. Finally, organizations should clearly communicate their commitment to diversity and act accordingly.

Occupational Segregation

Gender is strongly associated with job segregation with women's work and men's work being highly segregated according to both job types and organizational level. Occupational statistics demonstrate that there is a persistently unequal distribution of males and females throughout all ranges of occupations, and that this is an almost worldwide phenomenon. Males and females are both over-represented in particular organizational roles and levels of authority. Men tend to be highly concentrated in the higher-ranking professions, while women tend to be over-represented in the lowest-ranking and lowest paid professions in the workforce. This segregation of women into less prestigious and lower-ranked jobs also decreases their chances of being promoted and their access to insurance, benefits, and pensions.

A distinction can be made between horizontal segregation and vertical segregation. Horizontal segregation deals with the idea that men and women possess different physical, emotional, and mental capabilities. These different capabilities make the genders vary in the types of jobs they are suited for. Vertical segregation occurs as occupations are stratified according to the power, authority, income, and prestige associated with the occupation and women are excluded from holding such jobs.

Occupational and hierarchical segregation can be explained by individual choice, institutional structures, employer's choice, and "in-group" protectionism. That segregation is the result of individual choice is debatable, since institutional influences can constrain individual choice to such an extent that the idea of choice is simply the outcome of institutionally patterned actions. Segregation is often attributed to the processes of employer choice and active discrimination in hiring practices and can also be explained as a result of the power of "in-groups" to prohibit the admission of "out-group" members.

Gender Discrimination

The law recognizes four forms of gender discrimination: direct sex discrimination, sexual harassment, indirect sex discrimination, and victimization.

Direct sex discrimination is the less favorable treatment of a woman based on her sex.

Sexual harassment is defined as unwanted behavior that takes place simply based on gender, with the purpose of, or having the effect of, violating the person's dignity, or it creates an intimidating, hostile, degrading, humiliating, or offensive environment.

Indirect sex discrimination occurs when an employer applies a provision, criterion, or practice equally to both women and men that puts one sex at an unfair disadvantage. Because more women than men have family responsibilities and wish to work part-time, a policy that everyone has to work full-time can amount to indirect sex discrimination as it would put women at a particular disadvantage.

Victimization occurs when one is treated less favorably than others because he/she makes a complaint of discrimination or supports someone else to do. If you are denied promotion or training or are moved away from your usual workplace because of your involvement in a complaint of sex discrimination, this may be considered victimization.

Gender discrimination, like other forms of discrimination can lead to a decrease in job satisfaction, productivity, motivation, and performance, while it might increase absenteeism, turnover, and conflict. If gender discrimination is communicated outside the organization, it might damage its corporate image as well as run the risk of a lawsuit.

Pay Inequity

Wage discrimination is the discrepancy of wages between two groups due to a bias towards or against a specific trait with all other characteristics of both groups being equivalent. Women are paid less than men with the same qualifications, work experience, and having the same position. The pay inequity between men and women differs from country to country but ranges from 10% to 60%.

Career Interruptions

Pregnancy and maternity leave are issues that only concern women, making them prone to discrimination based on this matter. Common forms of this type of discrimination are not being hired or promoted when pregnant or being at an age where pregnancy is likely to happen in the near future, being fired or demoted after informing an employer of one's pregnancy, or being fired after one's maternity leave as a result of an expected loss in productivity.

Leadership Style

A trend towards flattening organizations, globalization, and a change more feminine organizational values can be identified, asking for a different leadership style. Men are thought to have a competitive, authoritative, transactional leadership style, compared to women who seem to place more emphasis on communication, empathy, relationships, advanced intermediary skills, interpersonal skills, and a soft approach to handling people. Although the feminine, transformational leadership style is getting recognized and valued, many organizations still embrace a "male-oriented" management style, where direct and aggressive behavior is the norm. However, when women embrace this style, they are frequently labeled as "bossy" and "pushy," whereas men using the same behaviors are labeled "leaders." Women report the perception that if they adopt a "feminine" managerial style, they run the risk of being viewed as ineffective, and if they adopt a "masculine" style, they will be criticized for not being feminine.

Disabled Colleagues in International Business

During the past few decades employers and government authorities have made increasing attempts to advance the participation and integration of disabled people in working life. This ranges from government legislation to company training programs for disabled people and company recruitment strategies targeting disabled job seekers.

However, barriers for employees with a disability still exist and workplace accommodations are difficult to implement as a result of the diversity within this group of employees.

Barriers for Employees With a Disability

Disabilities is an umbrella term, covering impairments, activity limitations, and participation restrictions. An impairment is a problem in body function or structure, an activity limitation is a difficulty encountered by an individual in executing a task or action, while a participation restriction is a problem experienced by an individual in involvement in life situations. Thus disability is a complex phenomenon, reflecting an interaction between features of a person's body and features of the society in which he or she lives. It should be stressed, however, that having a disability also carries a social stigma from which employees with a disability suffer because they fail to meet the norms of society.

Furthermore, social and material barriers also continue to exclude disabled people from the labor market and segregate disabled employees in work organizations. However, the small proportion of disabled people that is employed in paid work is rarely to be found in professional and managerial occupations. They are mostly to be found in semi-skilled and unskilled occupations, routine clerical and personal service work, and they are overrepresented in the rising numbers working from home.

Legislation

Discrimination based on disability is prohibited. In several countries laws have been voted for that state that organizations have to hire a certain percentage of employees with a disability. Organizations that feel to meet these quotas have to pay a fine. Although the percentage of employees with a disability is rising, there are still many organizations that prefer to pay instead of hiring disabled employees.

Workplace Accommodations

Organizations try to improve the employment opportunities of disabled people by increasing awareness about disability and disabled employees through making training about disability compulsory for colleagues and/or clients so they will feel comfortable interacting with disabled employees and by providing adaptations to disabled individuals or groups. The problem is that employees with a disability are an extremely heterogeneous group. The organizational adjustments to accommodate disability are costly, and initiatives aimed at enabling one disabled person may disable another.

Perception of Age in International Business

The workplace is aging. The active workforce is decreasing while the retired workforce increases rapidly. Many countries have decreased the official retirement age during the economic growth and the changing welfare philosophy of the past few decades. However, in the light of the aging population, this and other work-related issues are currently open to debate and it is clear that people will have to continue working for more years than in the past. However, although governments are taking measures to encourage people to keep on working, the current facilities and mentality at the workplace are not yet adapted to such a dramatic increase of older employees.

While age is valued and respected in certain Asian countries, it is viewed rather negatively in Europe where age discrimination is a serious issue.

Age Discrimination

Discrimination can be defined as the actions arising from institutions and individuals that disproportionately and systematically harm members of socially marginalized groups. Ageism or age discrimination is described as a process of systematic stereotyping of and discrimination against people because they are old or young, just as racism and sexism accomplish this for skin color and gender.

Age discrimination is based on the perception and attitudes people have regarding older employees. Clearly, these perceptions are quite negative. Older employees are believed to be less flexible and innovative, more resistant towards change, less motivated and energetic and less willing to take training opportunities, learn new skills, or new technology. As a result, older employees have fewer economic opportunities and therefore remain the most underrepresented group in the labor market. The only positive characteristics that are attributed to older employees are that they are seen as loyal and reliable.

Age discrimination has been linked to many negative psychological and organizational outcomes, like stress, distress, and functional limitations, lower job security, lower chances of promotion or receiving bonuses, reduced self-esteem, job satisfaction, job performance, affective organizational commitment, job involvement, and feelings of personal control.

Furthermore, older employees sometimes internalize the ageist assumptions and beliefs of others where they work, which influence their own attitudes and expectations. The perception of older employees that their accomplishment do not lead to career advancement as a result of these prejudices can have a negative influence on their motivation, thereby validating the stereotypes held by managers.

Age discrimination is high in someone's 20s, drops in the 30s, and peaks in the 50s. Age discrimination also interacts with other forms of discrimination, like gender, race, and class. It seems that women disproportionately experience age discrimination at the workplace, being doubly disadvantaged.

Workplace Accommodations

Many older employees wish to continue working if only their specific skills, knowledge, and experiences would get recognized and respected. Although many negative stereotypes exist about older employees, they do bring different values, skills, experiences, and ways of working to the work floor. Older employees have expressed the wish to transfer their knowledge and skills to younger employees, occupying a different social role in the organization such as being a mentor or a trainer. Facilities to reduce physically hard work are also appreciated as well as more flexibility, freedom, and autonomy regarding the execution of tasks, their working hours and the wish to balance work and personal life.

Using This Information

Diverse organizations are more productive when they manage to use this characteristic as an asset instead of fighting it as if it was a liability.

Working with minorities of any sort may be difficult for someone who is not used to it, because the exercise indeed represents a challenge to be overcome. The same way it must have been difficult for primary school teachers to switch from one-gender schools into coeducational ones, or the same way it must have been difficult to deal with female managers at some point in the twentieth century, it is still very difficult for teams to work with those who are different in some way.

This chapter should provide tools on how to deal with diversity in order to turn it to business advantage. Not because it is socially responsible, but because it can generate profit, enhance fairness, and greatly contribute to innovation and creativity.

Exercise

Reflect upon the social and economic cost of not promoting a diverse workplace.

CHAPTER 10

Intercultural Perceptions on Ethics

Contextualizing Background Information

The term "*ethics*" originated in the word "*ethos*," which means "*customs*." The word "*moral*" or "*morality*," which is usually used interchangeably with "*ethics*," derives from the Latin word "*more*," which could equally be translated as "*customs*."

Ethics, as well as morality has therefore been understood as the customary way to do things, probably, as opposed to the "sneaky" or marginal way of doing things. Customs are therefore supposed to be "the right way" to act and react and this definition has undoubtedly helped in developing frameworks for action in all cultures since ancient times.

The mere etymology of the word "ethics" therefore suggests that when dealing interculturally there might be misperceptions. If what is "ethical" is what is "customary" and "customs" are—by definition—culturally determined, then what is culturally conceived as "ethical" in one culture may well be considered as "unethical" by another.

The fact that it is commonly accepted to justify a behavior by saying "everyone does it here," supports our suspicion that people from different parts of the world may see "right" and "wrong" from different perspectives and the consequences of this may be quite relevant.

In this chapter we will explore different views on ethics from the angle of different cultural frameworks. We shall first explore some major objections to business ethics from the viewpoint of different cultural traditions, then we will confront the main modern business ethics paradigms from diverse perspectives, and we will elaborate on cultural relativism in particular with regard to specific business-related issues, such as nepotism, corruption, presents and bribes, and environmental concerns.

Objections to Business Ethics

Psychological Egotism

The first objection to business ethics to be treated is psychological ego-tism. According to this philosophy, taking people's interests into consideration when it could be contradictory to the enterprise's profitability is bad, and even unethical because it is in the nature of each person to protect him/herself first without caring for any others, and this attitude should therefore apply to business entities as well as to individuals to reach fairness.

This self-centered view is not perceived as negative; on the contrary, it is understood as the basis of progress. Within this framework, the role of the leader (either the business leader, or the national leader, or a leader of any sort) becomes therefore to manage interests making sure that they compatibilize in such a manner that the common good or the specific good of the company is reached. But it would be unrealistic to expect people to behave as something they are not—genuinely generous creatures—and therefore it would be dangerous to respond to egoism with altruism.

This psychological egotism objection would certainly be unwelcome to most South East Asian collectivist cultures. The role of the company in these cultures is to protect people working in them, so having to work under a rule that suggests "each one for himself" instead of guaranteeing protection to all would create an enormous amount of discontent. In the psychological contract between most Japanese companies and their employees it is mutually agreed that there is an exchange of protection for loyalty, which honors both parts of the deal.

In fact, the act of manifesting protection underlines the hierarchical distance: the boss protects and the fact that he or she has the capacity to do so underlines his or her status. Another example of a less collective culture with the same logic is France. Each level within the French hierarchy has specified roles to fulfill, and that of the higher ones is to make sure that the lower ones are safe. In return, there is not just loyalty, but the much socially appreciated feeling that one has "cared" for those who are below and therefore the higher position is legitimized.

The psychological egotism objection would find it difficult to survive in feminine cultures, because it is inspired in the quite ruthless idea that each one should care for his/her own interests without assuming any social role beyond that of fulfilling the interests of the powerful.

Particularist, synchronic cultures would find it hard to make efforts that go beyond the minimum to keep their jobs under such premises. Assuming the basic rule for all social and economic exchanges is based on the "you do this for me, I do this for you" principle, a world in which "each one is for himself and by himself" could sound disappointing and hurtful, and quite unfair. In these circumstances, in which there is no chance for trading favors, employees would end up doing the minimum with apathy and no passion, and employers would pay the minimum without caring about the personal circumstances or situation of their employees.

People from external locus of control cultures would react to the principles of psychological egotism with surprise and disgust. Immediately, they would wonder how such a system could be sustainable, as to them, most of the situations in life are beyond our control and therefore everyone should be ready to help others in a crisis to expect the same in return. How would a company in a crisis expect a positive, helpful attitude from its employees if they do not act the same way towards them?

Within an "achieving" cultural context, the psychological egotism principles could be perceived as an incentive to compete for the best position, even if the company is an entity that appears stronger than the individual. In an ideal flexible market, in which the most valuable employees are a rare asset, not owing loyalty can be perceived as a competitive advantage to the employee. In ascribed cultural contexts, on the other hand, such thinking could either be perceived as a potential threat to the status of the highly positioned (who gain legitimacy through charitable giving of what they do not actually need, which is typically French) or as the normal way things are (employees are lazy and do the minimum, therefore they need to be paid the minimum, which is typically Hispano-Latin American).

Machiavellianism

A similar objection is based on the writings of Machiavelli in *The Prince*,[1] and assumes that in order to succeed in business, it is necessary to deceive, lie, cheat, manipulate, use people, alter evidence, lobby, make alliances, generate obligations towards subordinates, gain control over rare resources, and so forth.

According to this view, all sorts of cheating are allowed at any game implying power, because this is what is required to be victorious. In business, as in war, there are winners and losers, and those who do not deceive, lose. Therefore, it is part of business to hurt others.

The Machiavellian objection might not be very compatible with the idea of "good" and "bad" of feminine cultures (perhaps with the exception of high power distance feminine cultures). In these cultures, in which business meetings are longer because consensus should be reached and every aspect of every decision needs to be discussed, manipulation would not serve in the long run, and if discovered would be generally rejected.

In particularist cultures, manipulation is something rather acceptable. As it is common to progress and to achieve objectives through the mutual giving of favors, it appears as normal to generate circumstances in which "the powerful" could owe in order to have him or her feel the need to give back later on. Someone from a universalist culture would see this differently, as when receiving a gift or a favor, he might gladly accept it without having the impression there are any strings attached.

Universalist people (Germans, for instance) would not support the idea of cheating or using people. Brits might digest it, though as if they see it as the only means available to have people do good (i.e., accept unavoidable, but unwanted change, for example), without the use of violence or getting into a conflict situation that would be bad for everyone in the long term.

In high power distance cultures, manipulating, deceiving, and cheating can be perceived by the ranked members of society as a legitimate way to calm less privileged ones down and prevent them from creating a fuss, going on collective strikes, or generating conflict that could get out of hand. The normal and even acceptable general state of "order" could then be reestablished and the system could then continue to operate (for the benefit of the ruling-uneven, unequal class society).

Long-term orientation cultures would find it hard to cope with cheating and manipulation, because for them, forgiving and forgetting is rare. Whatever is done to someone is kept in memory for a long time. On the other hand, much more is tolerated and excused before a business relationship is broken forever, because of the value attributed to its generation and construction.

The Machiavellian view on ethics requires in many cases a very high context communication style. Words, movements, suggestions, references to past events, roles, dissimulated threats, and false compliments are useful ingredients to the whole Machiavellian scenario, and therefore they can be more effective when applied by those with the habit of sugarcoating words. It is also typical of emotional cultures, in which emotional manipulation can often be quite dramatic and explicit. A neutral negotiator can be easily mislead by a partner who slams the door to suddenly come back with an offer, or by a female executive who cries in public to obtain what she wants.

People from achieving cultures may be interested in using some of the artifacts put forward by Machiavellianism in order to justify their access to success, which might grant them enough social respect to compensate for the eventual bad image resulting from a corrupted action. Ascribers may not need to call for Machiavellian actions to access power, as it is given to them automatically by the system. On the other hand, they might have to learn tricks to defend themselves from mischievous attempts at taking profit by less privileged counterparts. This may be one of the reasons why in ascribed cultures, people tend to communicate only with those of their same status or higher and ignore those of lower status. Lower status people are always looked down upon with disrespect, but above all, with suspicion of abuse.

Legal–Moral

The third argument against business ethics is more of a limitation than an objection as such. It states that whatever is legal cannot be unethical and therefore all moral reasoning about what is right or wrong is delegated to decision makers in parliaments, courts of justice, and the like.

This view is highly preferred by universalists, who espouse a natural preference for established general rules to be applied with as few exceptions as possible. Particularists, on the other hand, would find this objection revolting, as the legal norms could well have been established by a corrupted elite, and therefore be extremely biased to say the very least (and highly corrupted to be more specific).

Highly positioned powers from power distant cultures and favored members of ascribed societies may like this argument for as long as they can manipulate the law through lobbying and/or connections. They may also choose to apply the rule when it is convenient to them and disregard it when it will not be to their interest.

Individuals from external locus of control cultures would find this restriction of little logic, as to them unexpected events could easily distort the spirit of the law or a law that once made sense would not make sense at another moment. For example, a rule imposing a health check for a now eradicated disease of all people arriving in the United States by boat from Europe might have been of use in the nineteenth century, but it would be ridiculous to apply it nowadays. Constitutions and legal paperwork are full of these out-of-date legislations, which are often exclusively applied when agendas completely alien to the spirit of the law are in the minds of high decisions makers.

People from achieving cultures may have interests in playing with the limits and the interpretations of the law to achieve their goals, and if information on all legislation in place is not uniformly distributed across ascribed societies, it would become very easy to mislead lower classes into their own exploitation, as they may not be completely aware of their legal rights and could therefore not be able to defend themselves appropriately, even in cases in which the law would be on their side.

Agency Arguments

This objection is based on Milton Friedman's[2] study condemning the doctrine of social responsibility. According to Friedman, managers owe loyalty to their companies and it is their duty to use the stockholders' resources to maximize their profit exclusively. In Friedman's view, any action aiming at promoting the common good that has no direct implications on the increase of profitability for the enterprise can be considered as dishonest and must be sanctioned.

The condemnation of the doctrine of corporate social responsibility can certainly be objected from a feminine point of view, as often decisions that benefit companies have serious implications on individual people who are much more vulnerable than a corporation. In fact, when a company goes bankrupt or suffers from a lawsuit, shareholders can only lose the value of their stock, whereas workers can lose their livelihood, their careers, their reputation, and so forth.

Collectivist cultures from South East Asia and high power distant cultures acting under the logic of honor would probably have a similar thought: the interdependent exchange of loyalty for protection is an integral part of the psychological tacit contract between a company and its employees. Employees would not give their best of themselves unless they feel there is reciprocity in the commitment to stand for the satisfaction of their subsistence needs whenever necessary.

Individualistic, achieving, specific, short-term orientation cultures would be a bit keener to support this objection, as companies embracing masculine values of independence and "let the best one win" attitudes are often arenas in which people with high ambitions can develop faster and further.

Bodies of Thought on Business Ethics

Authors around the world have attempted to find ways to define ethical behavior and recipes to describe what good behavior is. In this portion of the chapter, we will briefly describe some of the most popular perspectives on ethics, even if our synthesis on the many and varied existing perspectives is not exhaustive.

Utilitarianism

This philosophy tries to measure the outcomes of each ethical decision in terms of benefits and drawbacks and then approve those that ensure the greatest benefit to the greatest number of people. It has been developed by Jeremy Bentham[3] (1748–1832) and John Stuart Mill[4] (1806–1873). From the utilitarian point of view, if an action produces more happiness than pain, then it is a good action.

Criticisms to this perspective are multiple, and complex when we measure them from a cross-cultural perspective.

In universalistic cultures, a universal measuring method that could determine what is good and what is bad out of a simple cost/benefit formula would certainly be welcome. The rule being clear and applicable almost mathematically, it would be perceived as fair and objective. In particularistic cultures, on the other hand, many objections would arise, such as who determined the formula, how can one measure good outcomes versus bad outcomes, and they would challenge not only the objectivity of the formula, but also its application in practice. For instance, if in a case of a war the cost was to be measured in terms of lives lost, a particularist would argue that not all lives are worth the same and that it would be inappropriate to create a scale to rank the worth of people's lives without being discriminatory in any way.

Collectivist cultures would be more inclined to favor such a measure, as in them, "the good of the many outweigh the needs of the few," whereas in individualistic cultures, each person is supposed to be in search of his/her own lives and ways to develop personally giving a secondary priority to the general outcome of any decision.

In feminine cultures, the ideas of utilitarianism would be accepted, for as long as immediate attention was to be paid to those suffering for the sake of the many. This view would be in way similar to that of long-term orientation cultures, with the difference being that in those, the ones being sacrificed today could find their comfort in the future because at a later time others would be expected "to take the bullet" in return.

People from high uncertainty avoidance cultures might well like the idea of having a formula to determine what is and what is not ethical, as such a guideline would release them from the painful duty of having to decide and risk making a mistake in the process. In high power distance cultures, if the benefit of the many was to challenge the privileges of the elite, this could at some stage become undesirable for the high classes, but very rewarding for the lower ones. In fact, it is not rare to see this principle apply in high power distance cultures, with a slight nuance, though. If the many are to be damaged very little and the small, insignificant sacrifice of the many was to generate a huge, visible benefit for the few, then the decision may even be considered as desirable. For instance, if every citizen was to pay a 0.1 tax to offer an item to their country representative that would be conspicuous, then this might be considered as acceptable... for as long as they have the hope of being rewarded with loyalty and protection on other occasions. Or to prove to foreigners or strangers that their representatives are wealthy and strong (which should reflect somehow on their own image).

Deontology

This philosophical perspective (from Greek "Deo Mai" or "I must") is based on Immanuel Kant's[5] (1724–1804) "Categorical Imperative," or set of commandments to be respected at any time by everyone, no matter the circumstances. The basic rule could be formulated as "do unto others as you would have done unto yourself" and never treat others as a means to an end.

This is the ideal of a universalist world in which all the rules can be obeyed by following one precept or a series of them. The deontological ideal of the world would very much suit the uncertainty avoiders, as a simple checklist would suffice to free them from the complexities of having to decide what is right and what is wrong, while protecting them from the risk of a mistake.

From a particularistic viewpoint, or for instance, from an external locus of control one, living by a list of principles could only result in lack of flexibility, either because life is too complicated to be schematized or compressed into a few commandments or because the human mind is not capable of directing, predicting, or stereotyping all possible foreseeable or unforeseeable situations.

Stakeholder Approaches

This trend in business ethics was born as a reaction to Milton Friedman's objections to ethics in business. Indeed this view favors the understanding of a company as morally bound to respect and balance the interests of not just the shareholders, but of all stakeholders: employees, regional development agencies, shareholders, consumers, suppliers, the environment, and so forth. Contrary to utilitarianism, these more modern approaches see the company's role as that of a social actor with responsibilities including a fair distribution of wealth and externalities across its stakeholders. This way, it is not just the majority that sees the benefits of the enterprise operations, but everyone is supposed to, in particular the minorities involved.

Universalists would see in this approach a fair option where there is an official system of distribution in place that is respected across the board. Particularists, on the other hand, would see in it an opportunity for manipulation and for the benefit of those who are more powerful anyway.

The stakeholder approach is very popular amongst feminine cultures, which appreciate its capacity to satisfy the needs of the powerful without leaving the fragile aside, and it suits people from high power distant cultures, because in them the unprivileged can certainly have their minimum needs covered and the powerful find it easier to avoid confrontation.

Achievers criticize this approach very often by terming it an obstacle in the natural ambition of humans, who have to pay for those who do not make comparable efforts, and individuals from masculine societies may think similarly.

In long-term orientation cultures, if well communicated, the stakeholder approach can be understood as a series of investments in the future; but in short-term orientation cultures, it may be perceived as a waste of resources, an opportunity for bribery, or the instauration of marginal give/give situations.

Character Virtue

This view promotes the observation and development of the manager or director at individual level, assuming that someone who is basically a good person, can be good, do good, act good, whereas someone who does not have a certain series of characteristics will not.

This perspective focuses on the person, rather than on the system, ignoring whether or not someone would follow his or her values to the extreme when put under pressure.

Particularists would agree with this view, in the sense that a good person may sometimes need to act bad if the circumstances force him/her to do so, but this is part of human nature. What is important is that the person has an inclination to act good, and that is enough, because if such is the case, most of the outcomes of his or her actions will be positive. Universalists would argue that there is no formal way to determine that a person may be officially declared as "good" or "bad," even if in many universalist societies it is customary to invent or make up approximate ways to determine whether a person is good or bad. For instance, graduates from very strict schools, PhD holders, notaries, and so forth are considered in many societies (in ascribed ones in particular) as virtuous people.

Synchronics would argue that it is impossible to determine whether a person deserves trust or is "good" without having known him or her for a long time. It is through longitudinal analysis of their actions that one can be absolutely sure of someone else's character. The same argument would work for people from diffuse cultures as well, who suppose it is only after a stranger has passed a series of unofficial tests that he or she can be welcome to the inner circles of friendship.

Cultural Relativism in Ethics

As debated in the previous pages, it would be difficult to create one generic global set of rules that would determine what is right and what is wrong.

Even if Peter Singer maintains that traditions around the world tend to converge, and numerous studies have predicated that every major tradition (Judaism, Christianity, Confucianism, Hinduism, Buddhism, and Islam) teaches the golden rule "treat others the same way you would like to be treated",[6] still it would be naïve to expect all different cultures to share a common ideology on what is good and what is bad.

Cultural relativism suggests that "When in Rome, do like the Romans," meaning that executives should adapt to local uses and customs and should ignore personal or rules applicable back home when operating abroad.

This viewpoint supports for example, actions that are condemnable by law in many Western cultures, such as bribery, child employment, pollution, and so on, but that are common practice in other areas under the argument that competition may take over, acting like locals, and markets would be lost. On the other hand, local religious rules, dress code requirements for females, and other behavioral impositions found abroad could sometimes block the fluidity of business if ignored or not respected.

Donaldson and Dunfee[7] have produced a partial attempt to find a balanced solution between the "reef of relativism" on one side and the "reef of colonial morality" on the other while creating the integrative social contracts theory, which is a set of priority norms to be applied when dealing internationally.

Our own perspective in this sense is that whereas it would be difficult to apply or to impose rules, or else to accept and apply local requirements that seem too strict, the secret consists in finding ways to call for the common spirit of the norms and find common ground. Understanding the origins of rules and sharing them may be a step forward and making a difference, even when this means accepting that some degree of flexibility may be required, is in many cases the solution.

A great deal of patience and enormous emotional intelligence is required, though, to ensure common ground based on other considerations than superficial practices, but it is precisely that extra mile that differentiates outstanding international business players from mediocre ones.

Using This Information

More often than not, it is easy to judge other people's conduct out of context through stereotyping, in the sense of "Oh... you know, those people from XXX always cheat/don't keep their word/always think for themselves/never know how to behave/ do not know what friendship really is about...."

Whenever business is talked, money is talked. And wherever money is involved, ethical questions appear. A rounded global manager and/or businessperson will certainly be able to understand where other people's principles may come from. This does not necessarily mean that he or she will have to abide by them, or to practice them, but at least know what is happening and be better prepared to react in the best possible way.

No matter how much effort is being put into designing a global code of ethics, acceptable and practicable by every culture in the world (and some researchers are currently working very seriously in this area), it will be very difficult to find an objective answer to every dilemma.

The preceding text will at least provide the main ideological positions in the matter and hopefully work as a guide to those wondering about the best way to resolve specific issues in different occasions.

Simulated Exercise

On an Excel worksheet, produce a simulated table crossing different ethical perceptions and objections and frameworks for cultural analysis and complete it.

	Psychological Egotism	Machiavel-lianism	Legal Moral	Etc.
Individualists/ collectivists	Collectivists do not favor its lack of consideration for all members of the group. Company does not look like a "family." Individualists consider a company a social player, so are more likely to accept it.	Collectivists find it cold and insensitive. Individualists may object to the unfairness of the system.	Collectivists may object to the origin of the norms (i.e. could be a corrupted government). Individualists may want to rely on fair rules for a fair game.	
Feminine/ masculine				
Uncertainty avoidance				
Etc.				

CHAPTER 11

Cross-Cultural Teamwork

Veronica Velo and Andrew Barron

The aim of this chapter is to apply the previously discussed frameworks for cultural analysis to predict and be able to deal with the most common problems relating to working in or with international teams.

Departing from a model describing different types of teams, we will develop on what would be the right attitude when these teams are composed of people from different cultural backgrounds, thinking, feeling, and acting according to their own mental programmings.

Contextualizing Background Information

Driven by the rise of the multinational enterprise and new technologies, cross-cultural teams are a common feature of international business. A cross-cultural team is a small number of people from different cultural backgrounds, working towards a common purpose. A key characteristic of a cross-cultural team is cultural diversity, which relates to the degree of cultural difference represented in a team.

Cultural diversity differs across cross-cultural teams. Essentially, the degree of a team's cultural diversity depends on two things. First, it depends on the cultural distance between the members of the team. Here, cultural distance relates to the perceived distance between two cultures: the more characteristics that cultures have in common, the smaller the cultural distance, the fewer characteristics that cultures have in common, the greater the cultural distance.

Cultural diversity in teams also depends on the number of cultures represented in the team. The more cultures included in a team, the more diverse it is going to be. We can differentiate between token

teams, bicultural teams, and multicultural teams. In a token team, all
the members but one come from the same national culture. Bicultural
teams consist of members representing two distinct cultures. The members of truly multicultural teams come from three or more cultural
backgrounds.

Cross-cultural teamwork is not restricted to transnational teamwork, meaning teamwork between people from different countries.
Cross-cultural teams can also be understood in a wider sense. As
explained earlier in this book, we can talk about different layers of
cultures. So, below the national level, we can also see regional cultures,
industry cultures, corporate cultures, and occupational cultures. In
this sense, we could feasibly talk about cross-cultural teamwork within
individual companies. Figure 11.1 points out potential sources of miscommunication in pluricultural teams, through examples based on collectivist versus individualist cultures.

Take the example of a project team established by a company to
market a new product. The team might bring together representatives
from the finance department and the sales department. The members
of the finance department might be careful and conservative in terms of
spending. By contrast, the members of the sales department are likely to
be keen to spend more money as this may result in more sales. So, these
two distinctive departments bring their own cultural baggage to the team.
The finance department appears to be more averse to risk than the sales
department.

	INDIVIDUALISTS	COLLECTIVISTS
Examples	USA, France, NL	Brazil, Japan
Way of defining onself	Through individual achievements	Through appartenance to the group
Relationships	Short term	Long term
Welfare	Individual	Group
Values	Accomplishment	Harmony, Unity, Loyalty

Transnational teams will work differently than monocultural ones

*Figure 11.1. Potential sources of miscommunication in
pluricultural teams.*

Types of Teams

In her article "Managing your Team," published by *Harvard Business Review* in 1994, Linda Hill[1] put forward three different types of teams, calling on sports metaphors. The intercultural factor has a different impact on each one of the following types of teams, as the required interactions and the dynamics vary in intensity and in frequency.

Basketball Teams

Hill called the first type she identified a "Basketball team," because in it everyone does his/her job independently, working "on" the team, as opposed to "as" a team. It is the typical case of factory's production lines (Taylor style) or a surgical team performing an operation in a theatre.

Because even if the jobs are interdependent, they still are independent; in this type of team it is easy to measure individual performance and this leads to less conflict because the level of interaction is lower. In this sense, this way of operating is preferred by achievers, masculine cultures, and individualists, because they see in it a chance to show their capacity and shine when being pointed out as the stars of the endeavor.

People from high uncertainty avoidance cultures also prefer this system, where the norms are clearly indicated through job descriptions and it is easy to use the operations manual to defend oneself when something goes wrong. Because the basketball team is very well structured, it suits the power distant, and the ascribers, because they like the hierarchies that the controls that are necessary to implement this system of work impose.

Neutrals may like it as well, the same as universalists, because the level of conflict is reduced by setting of profit units. If everyone knows what his/her duties are and it is visible when someone did not comply with the norm, then there is little room for misunderstanding or mutual blame. The "norm" can easily apply to everyone.

American Football Teams

The second type of team that was identified was the American football team. In it, players do their job "as" a team (as opposed to "on" a team), as if they had a common score of music to be followed. There is a strong feeling of team spirit and belonging in this type of team, in which every one has an important contribution to make. On the other hand, each one of the members must subordinate to the interests of the group, and individual contribution is difficult to identify. The victory is a common victory, and so is the defeat. Unless there are very strong ties and commitment to the whole, it is very hard to motivate individually.

This type of team is very common in collectivist ascribed cultures, where individual achievement is perceived as a motive for envy and shame, rather than as the basic requirement for professional progression.

Uncertainty avoidant cultures may find it hard to accept this type of work, because in times of conflict, it would be more difficult to identify the causes of low productivity or of malfunctions, so a lack of method to identify actions on a particular basis may sound disruptive and cause concern.

Individuals from high power distant cultures may appreciate this type of team as long as it occurs within the same level of the hierarchy. For example, in Japan, this type of team has allowed the flourishing of very successful production methods, such as total quality management or just in time, because everyone involved in the operations assumed a role to play and went along with it very seriously. The failure of a company was understood as everyone's failure regardless of their level within the hierarchy. Nevertheless, the hierarchy was always seriously maintained, and relationships between the higher caste and the lower ones are strongly based on trust, loyalty, and honor.

This type of game requires a strong commitment between members, and being ready to "give one for the team" more often than not, which makes it much more appealing to members of diffuse cultures (in which every action affects all levels of life and therefore it makes sense to "give more than what the contract says"). Also, this type of team dynamics is very compatible with long-term orientation cultures, because constituting a team that works well and in which "all for one and one for all" is the rule, takes time. People from achieving, sequential cultures would feel very disappointed if having to work under such a rule, because it would seem quite frustrating to them having to put their egos in second place.

In emotional cultures, the fact of having to put feelings at stake in every aspect of life makes this team style a good arena for devoting passion to the work done together, but communication needs to be handled with care, because the loss of harmony could cause serious disruptions to the proceedings and work outcomes; so high context exchanges need to take place, not to have anyone be vexed or offended by coworkers.

Tennis Doubles Teams

The third type of team identified by Hill was the tennis doubles team. Within this arrangement, only the team performs. Players just contribute to the common score. Team members cover their teammates, adjusting as necessary to their talents and weaknesses and acting according to the demands of the game.

This type of team is very productive when well organized, but it requires collaboration, commitment, and trust. Members need to have been trained together for some time in order to be able to work smoothly together. Within this arrangement, hierarchies matter more than anything else.

This sort of arrangement suits particularistic people, as there is trust involved. There is a need for quick reaction, therefore the checking for universal rules to be applied could take precious time that ought to be otherwise used.

It is difficult to think in terms of short-term orientation when it comes to having tennis doubles teams work well, mainly because it becomes necessary to develop knowledge of how the other person plays as well as ways to guess what the other person is thinking before action takes place.

Communication in general takes place implicitly, so the preferred communication style is high context. The tennis doubles teams would certainly suit achievers, as long as the victories allow for them to shine individually as well; but is not good for power distants, because quick reactions are expected and this is not possible to achieve when hierarchical procedures come to block natural developments instead of reinforcing them.

New Ways of Working

Postindustrial societies are more and more involved with new ways of working, which require the constitution and dissolution of teams on a

Type of Team	Description	Pros	Cons
Baseball team (or Ford's line, or surgical team)	• Each one does his job. • People play ON the team, but not AS a team.	• Easy to measure individual performance. • Low interdepend- ence (less conflict)	• No communication. • Less synergy. • Inflexible. • Not that many repetitive tasks required nowadays.
Football team (or orchestra, or emergency room staff trying to save a heart-attack patient)	• Players play "AS a team". • Common "score of music" to be followed.	• Team spirit • Feeling of belonging to a structure.	• Team members must subordinate to the team (difficult to motivate individually).
Tennis doubles team (or improvisa- tional ensemble or self-managed manu- facturing team)	• Only the team performs, indi- vidual members just contribute. • Team members cover their teammates, adjusting as necessary to their team- mate's talents and weaknesses and gauging demands of the game.	• Very produc- tive if well organized.	• Requires commit- ment, trust, and collaboration. • Members have to be trained together for some time before they can fully function according to this model. • Not suitable for "hierarchically oriented" people.

short-term basis. Those teams tend to be led by generalists, who coordi-
nate the work of specialists. For instance, to create a new drug to fight
cancer, a specialist manager will be called to lead a team consisting of a
well-known oncologist, a specialist in biotechnology, drug marketers, etc.
These specialists from anywhere in the world would get together around
the generalist to work on a specific project, which will soon after be dis-
solved. They may or may not work together again.

The new ways of working call for project orientation on very immediate and specific areas, and people involved in it need to be prepared to
act in a very specific way. Relationships are meant to be short-term and
communication needs to be explicit. Achievers may feel at ease as long as
they take tangible credit for the outcome.

These new ways of working are difficult to deal with for people with high power distance orientation and for uncertainty avoiders, because there is a need for quick reaction (which hierarchy would slow down) and there is no chance of blaming others: the risks need to be taken and the consequences follow on the team, not on individuals.

Collectivists, synchronics, and people from diffuse cultures generally feel uneasy within these arrangements, because of their impersonality. They find the coldness of the short-term groupings annoying and sad. Ascribers resent the lack of recognition that should come other than from achievements and universalists believe it is hard to function sometimes without specific rules to be followed.

Teams of Teams

Even if there are all types of teams in all cultures, and even if subcultures such as industry or company can influence the selected type of team more than national culture, it would be worthwhile analyzing what sort of problems could arise when people used to or preferring a particular type of team are forced either to change into another team framework or to merge with others who are used to working with a different type of team. How would a basketballer manage to play a doubles tennis team? How would a footballer score at basketball? How would any of these sports-businessmen score at new ways of working?

For instance, when having to work together, people used to operating "basketball style" may find those used to the "football style" casual, noisy, and disorganized. "Basketballers" would be looking for a set of tasks clearly identified, scheduled, and regulated, and to be performed individually. They would also be wanting to know what is expected from each person and how performance is to be assessed and compensated. "Footballers" would find "basketballers" annoying and bureaucratic, egoistic, and unfriendly.

Basketballers would also find the tennis players casual and disorganized, always wanting to do new things without following a procedure. Roles could change automatically without any previous discussion and the ball would just come and go too quickly for them to react in a rational and professional manner. Tennis players would find basketballers slow in reaction, boring, bureaucratic, and hierarchical.

If forced to work under the new ways of working, basketballers would be annoyed by the lack of structure and by the fact that they would have to make decisions on the spot, without following a specified procedure. Most probably, basketballers would dislike innovating or listening toothers, and would require a boss who is a specialist, not a generalist, because someone who does not know better than everyone else would hardly be legitimate as a proper superior.

When footballers interact with tennis players, both teams would appreciate the coordination and mutual support, but the latter would resent the lack of flexibility and coordination from the other side. Footballers might find tennis players cold and lacking a centralized structure or "common generalized feeling of belonging."

But footballers may find the hardest of times dealing with the new ways of working, because the huge feeling of belonging from years of working together and developing mutual trust would just not exist in this scenario. Footballers may find the fact of having to reunite and disintegrate groups on short notice quite annoying and sad. The fact that in the new ways of working individual achievement is valued and recognized would seem egoistic and naive for the group ambience to the footballers. People involved in the new ways of working would find footballers unproductive and oversensitive, and perhaps not very profit oriented, which would require some dynamism and responsiveness.

Finally, when confronting or trying to have tennis players adapt to the new ways of working, a problem may arise in terms of having to adapt to other players rather soon and then having to replace them with others on the next project. Tennis players would need time to adapt and get to

Advantages	Disadvantages
• Creativity • Possibility to invent new solutions • Less "groupthink" • Forces members to pay more attention to their colleagues	• More difficult to see situations in similar ways, understand them in similar ways, and act on them in similar ways • Diversity makes reaching agreement more difficult • Employees of the same culture trust each other more easily • Misperception, misinterpretation, misevaluation, miscommunication • Stress, ambiguity, complexity, confusion.

know their partners as much as possible before developing lasting work relationships that are to derive in sustained performance.

Identifying Cross-Cultural Teams

Below, employees talk about their experiences of working in multicultural environments. Some of the problems presented derive from national culture differences, others from differences in subcultures. Frameworks for cultural analysis and the types of teams described above help us identify the key issues and suggest avenues for resolution.

An American engineer working in Stuttgart

It's something I'd never admit to anybody here at work, but I really do feel happiest when I'm working on my own. I like to be in control, and I like to be rewarded for my individual efforts. I don't like the idea of my bonus being partly dependent on my colleagues' performance. For all I know, they could be spending their days taking endless coffee breaks.

This typical member of an individualistic, highly achieving culture would probably feel more at ease working under a "tennis" setting than under the "football" or the "basketball" environment he/she seems to have been pushed to join.

Probably his or her colleagues would not appreciate his/her disrespect of the norm (that perhaps would allow the coffee breaks) that bothers him/her because he/she feels that it prevents him/her from taking control (internal locus of control).

This engineer's supervisor should perhaps consider either finding a way to recognize the particular effort of the engineer, give him/her every opportunity to develop on his/her own and slowly introduce him/her to a different view which implies that sometimes coffee breaks have a meaning that goes beyond the mere refreshment (i.e., valuable information is usually disseminated informally during coffee breaks, conflicts arising from the need to work together are dealt with during coffee breaks, etc.).

Unless the supervisor makes an effort to reconcile the two ways of working, the company may be losing a valuable asset and/or the engineer could experience his/her stay in Stuttgart as a painful, horrible experience.

A PhD student from Brazil studying in Sweden

The working atmosphere here is pretty miserable, not at all like back home in Brazil. Everybody spends the whole day working alone in their offices. They keep their doors shut, so you feel bad knocking and asking for help. My colleagues never ask me what I'm doing. How the hell do people get anything done if they don't interact with each other?

In this case, we have a footballer suffering from having to play on his own sometimes. His collective, diffuse, synchronic, particularistic upbringing must be making it difficult for the Brazilian student to play a different game, perhaps more individualistic and above all, neutral.

A good student advisor would explain to this student that the tacit rule in Sweden is "We will help you when you need it, but you need to say it very clearly when you do," and that asking or offering help for things that one could do on one's own anyway is not considered as a relationship building exercise, but a sign of weakness.

Perhaps this student needs to be introduced to the Swedish social circles where fun takes place, as in specific societies there is a place for joy and a place for work. This Brazilian student may have only come across the second one and therefore he must feel very lonely, sad, and depressed. Unless someone at the university takes charge, the institution may well lose a good potential researcher who would just feel too homesick at some stage to finish his thesis.

An American software engineer, Santa Clara

The company hired a bunch of Puerto Rican software engineers. We went out of our way to avoid working with them. Everyone knows that the quality of education in Puerto Rico is poor compared to the States.

Here is the typical example of the non-sports (wo)man. And it is a very common case. No game can be played with someone who is not interested in playing.

Unless the supervisor or the human resources department of this company decides to firmly invest in training its American employees, they will have to face huge financial loses (in lawsuits, loss of productivity, loss of good workers, etc.).

Following the training, mingling exercises should take place, in which coworkers should talk about their experiences, their studies, and share knowledge.

A Brazilian on his experiences of working with Americans

Many times I felt I didn't have the words to say what I was thinking. When I had meetings with the Americans, they would always tend to take the lead, which was understandable but also disappointing because we were at the same level in the company. I had some very good questions to ask, but I just lacked the confidence to express myself.

This is the same case as above. Parochialism in business is the result of poor education most of the people who graduated before the Internet have been through. This statement may be controversial, but very few people who graduated before 1995 are ready to work internationally, simply because they did not have the opportunity to understand that intelligence is not the monopoly of any country at all and that in every nation there are excellent schools and professionals.

Lack of preparation to deal with international coworkers in this case would certainly lead to the loss of great ideas and the perpetuation of "groupthink" within the teams. The opportunity cost involved is just too huge to be absorbed. Any competitor who is able to better manage his/her human resources would profit from the situation to do better.

An American on her experiences of working in a Japanese team

One of the hardest lessons for me was learning that, when the Japanese say 'yes' they just mean 'I'm listening to you.'

When working within football teams, it is very important to keep harmony alive and to reinforce it by avoiding conflict at any cost. A football team with players who detest or boycott each other can never win.

For this American, communicating with high context must have been a challenge, because the answers would take longer to be understood. But they eventually would.

A Swede discusses designing products in a multicultural team

We traditionally carried out product design at our Stockholm headquarters. Once, we brought in an international team to discuss the design of a new allergy product. Due to extreme differences in opinion on what constitutes good medical practice, the team designed the new product with maximum flexibility to suit the requirements of each country. We later discovered that the greater flexibility was a huge advantage in developing and marketing a wide range of internationally competitive products.

Here is a team that managed to create a new rule for all to play. When taking advantage of diversity, instead of ignoring, drowning, or fighting it, they made the best out of it. This company would certainly be stronger, more innovative in the market, than the ones discussed above. The feminine characteristic of Sweden has certainly helped in having every member express themselves, rather than assume that only one view should be imposed on everyone participating.

A Brit talks about a team-building exercise organized by French colleagues

The whole team was taken out to the middle of the Arabian desert. When we reached our final destination—a tiny village in the middle of nowhere—we found a jeep, a map, and a note from a French manager giving us one week to find our way to Riyadh. What a complete waste of time! We were keen to start work on formulating strategy. We didn't have the time to be fooling around in the desert.

The Brits wanted to play tennis, or use new ways of working. The French were trying to build a football team. So the training for a football team was to put everyone in a hard situation and get them sort it out together. By the time everyone had reached Riyadh, the team would be expected to be solid.

There was no interest from the French to have the team members formulate strategies. Strategies are formulated in France by the top members of the hierarchy, not by the lower managers. The lower managers just need to get along and develop a sense of belonging that will lead to loyalty.

The predicted result of this experience is two teams within the team: the British talking English and the French talking French. The French will probably discuss the strategy to get to Riyadh (and not the company strategy), the Brits would probably be criticizing the French and using common sense to find some sort of camel somewhere or call a taxi from their mobile phones.

A French woman recalls a project kick-off meeting in Washington, DC

I found the whole experience disconcerting. We hardly had any time to introduce ourselves to each other. Within minutes of arriving at the hotel, we were expected to sit down and work closely with these apparent strangers on developing a new financial strategy.

The French lady wanted to play football, but in DC they were playing new ways of working. This is a very disappointing game for a person from a diffuse culture, who needs to know people before trusting them, and to trust them before working with them productively.

A German technician working in Dallas

The problems began in the planning phase of the project. I wanted to use my expertise to fully understand the problem we were addressing. Instead, I was given specific targets and was expected to reach them in a very short time indeed. But were these really the best targets that I could have been given? For the sake of speed, a thorough analysis of the problem did not take place. How are we expected to do quality work on this basis?

The German technician wanted to play basketball on a tennis court. Now he is complaining because his Armanis are covered with clay.

In order to react quickly in tennis courts, it is necessary to assess the situation very fast and to act half by hunch, half by strategy. This is why trial and error is the preferred way of learning in cultures like the United States.

The German way of thinking is very deductive: first comes thinking, then comes acting. But in a tennis court, analysis can mean paralysis, therefore it is much more convenient to adapt to a fast-reaction mode and go with the flow. And this can certainly be disruptive and disturbing to a German mind.

An American technician working in Stuttgart

We met to define our overall strategy. I was expecting a brief two-hour brainstorming session—we'd develop some general solutions, select the best ones, and delegate tasks. Instead, we were sat there for three full days. The Germans loved to see themselves as 'Volk der Dichter und Denker' (people of poets and thinkers). But we don't have to endlessly dispute everything and act like a bunch of little Immanuel Kants to get a product to market.

This is the same problem, the other way round. The tennis player found himself in a basketball court, before the game, discussing the strategy with his colleagues. He just did not see the point in doing that.

A German technician working in Dallas

I was always astonished to see how quickly my American team leader reached a decision. He briefly thought about a problem, announced his decision, and that was it. The other team members just accepted his decisions without ever questioning them. I came to the conclusion that working life in America is much more authoritarian than it is in Germany. This actually came as quite a surprise to me, as I wasn't expecting this.

Americans understand that sometimes reaction means no time for discussion. And in that case, the person who is considered as the most likely to make the least errors is the one expected to make assumptions and go for a trial.

Using This Information

One of the hardest tasks for international managers to perform is probably the management of intercultural teams. And the least technical, more values-sensitive the task, the harder it becomes for a manager to have a group to act in productive harmony.

Understanding that not all members of an intercultural team could be "playing the same game" could perhaps help their coach realize that there should be some rethinking of the basic rules to be done, some talks to be organized, and some follow up to be undertaken.

Exercise

Imagine a situation in which you are to manage an intercultural team comprising members with diverse perceptions on how to work. Propose solutions to make such a team uniform.

PART IV

The Future of Cross-Cultural Management

CHAPTER 12

Culture and Globalization

The aim of this concluding chapter is to review the history of globalization and predict the consequences of its immediate future development in order for executives to reflect on the potential consequences in a world that has been changing faster than ever before and will continue to do so geometrically in the years to come.

Contextualizing Background Information

The definition of the term "*globalization*" has evolved through the years, sometimes including a few notions in it that would afterwards be excluded and vice versa. In spite of all the variations in the construction of the concept, there are at least two common factors that have remained constant across the changing attempts to qualify the phenomenon, namely its origins as a natural step in history, and its unavoidability.

Indeed, researchers agree that worldwide situational characteristics such as relative global peace, the international flow of information, the reduction of trade barriers, the international spread of technology, and the evolution of global market segments have contributed to a complete change in the way trade takes place and this has impacted societies and intersociety links as well. In a nutshell, it is generally agreed that globalization is about a new way of trading without borders that originated out of the conjunction of different historical events and that cannot be stopped.

As an example, Toyne and Walters have defined globalization in 1989 as follows: "the process of focusing an organization's resources on the selection and exploitation of global market opportunities consistent with and supportive of its short and long-term strategic objectives and goals." Prior to that, Levin had already defined it in 1983 as the "convergence of the markets of the world," and Ohmae had already described the process as an "integrated way of production."

Below are several definitions of the cultural phenomenon.

Tom G. Palmer of the Cato Institute defines globalization as "the diminution or elimination of state-enforced restrictions on exchanges across borders and the increasingly integrated and complex global system of production and exchange that has emerged as a result.

Thomas L. Friedman has examined the impact of the "flattening" of the world, and argues that globalized trade, outsourcing, supply-chaining, and political forces have changed the world permanently, for both better and worse. He also argues that the pace of globalization is quickening and will continue to have a growing impact on business organization and practice.

It would be difficult to establish a precise date for the birth of the globalization phenomenon. Some authors would argue that in fact it had originated with trade itself, but as a matter of convenience, and to concentrate on the most influential portions of its historical evolution, we will only describe the main phases having shaped progress in international trade operations from the Second World War onwards.[1] In fact, since then, a series of stages have followed and it could be generally agreed that we still find ourselves in the midst of the events. In order to simplify the study of the evolution of globalization and its impact on culture, we will divide the history of the process into phases.

The first phase we consider is called "**Home**" because the basic trend at that point (immediately after the Second World War) consisted in simply exporting the excess production with no alterations or with just very simple ones. The main idea was to liquidate stocks or to accept orders of an existing product from abroad, but this product would be entirely designed and conceived for the local market. For example, a producer of chairs would manufacture them using local labor, and following specifications that would correspond to the demands of the local public. In case there was an excess of production, it would be sold abroad, but without taking into consideration any adaptations to the foreign public. Producers just "let" foreigners buy their product.

By the 1950s, inspired businesspeople realized that their expertise could be transformed into business opportunities abroad, and therefore they proceeded to the development of units in different locations, which functioned more or less independently, but that were designed to deserve each local market in which they operated. Because each unit would act domestically, but in different locations, this phase in the globalization process is called "**Multilocal.**" The added advantage of this method was that it allowed the expansion of operations in cases where the local market was saturated or to take advantage of opportunities elsewhere. To continue with the previous example, in this case, chairs would be produced in different places using local labor, designing them to satisfy the needs and tastes of the local markets and to be sold to the local people through the practice of local techniques and aiming at pleasing the local clients and customers.

In the 1960s, developments in travel and telecommunications technology enabled the first stages of global production, the outsourcing of processes and the importing of inputs from economically viable locations. This new way of production allowed progress into the standardization of goods, at a significantly lower price. Applied to the example of the chairs, in this stage a Swedish manufacturer would buy the wood from Finland, the design from Canada, do the assembly in Mexico, and then distribute the standardized product across the world. Due to the diversity and number of countries involved in the process, this phase is called "**International.**"

By the 1980s, the need for a differentiating factor became key to those wanting to compete on the cost battlefront. Those able to marry quality and low cost managed to gain competitive advantage and were therefore able to position themselves strategically. The main idea consisted in taking the multinational phase one step further by customizing the product or service to particular markets at the last step of their production. This way would ensure that cost conditions were met and that at the same time the offer would match the requirements of the local demand. In the case of chair production, the main processes would be universal (design and production procedures), but at the last points, slight alterations (size, color, distribution systems, etc.) would be made in order to adapt to specific preferences. Because of its intended capacity to meet the needs and wants of every segment, without sacrificing cost-saving standardization, this phase is called "**World**."

By the year 2000, economic blocks had relatively stabilized in terms of free circulation of goods and workforce, which accelerated the division of tasks into high versus low added value producing. Post-industrialized nations initiated a process of relocation of their manufacturing activities abroad, keeping the core competency at home, mainly concentrating on "brainwork" and replacing factories in foreign locations. Ecological issues start to gain importance in the minds of citizens and this increased sensitivity promoted the evolution and acceleration of the same dynamics. As creativity is considered as a key success factor in this phase, cross-cultural thinking is promoted and developed nations start to compete in the attraction and retention of the brightest minds across the globe. To continue with the same example, in this case the chair would be designed in Sweden by the best designers from everywhere in the world, produced in China and distributed using an American company. This phase is called "**Decentralized**."

The most recent developments in trade have allowed the development of networks of thought, which, distributed across the globe, act as the concentrators of know-how and creativity, which will then be applied in the production and marketing of goods wherever manufacturing takes place. Because the way of working implied in this new phase is much decentralized and operates through networks, it has been named "**Networked**." In this sense, thought occurs wherever the brains are located, which act as "centers of knowledge," operating in very small and reactive structures all over the world, which concentrate and dissolve as soon as the tasks and projects are accomplished.

The table below synthesizes the evolution of globalization since the Second World War providing main characteristics of each phase:

Phase	Description
Home (immediately following the Second World War)	• Producing for locals, exporting the rest, • Less product variety, • No interest in satisfying foreign needs, • It is up to the client to perform his/her own "customization," • Foreigners buy a product that is foreign to them.

(Continued)

(*Continued*)

Phase	Description
Multilocal phase (1950–1960)	• Tackling opportunities abroad by producing and selling abroad for foreign consumption, • Adaptation to each one of the local cultures in which the company is present, • From product orientation to market orientation, • Each subsidiary acts as a local company abroad, • Locals are sometimes unaware that the capital is foreign, • Customized products for local clients in each location.
International phase (1960s)	• Price becomes the key differentiating factor, because many companies produce almost the same, • Low cost becomes a priority over cultural preferences, • The cheaper, the better, • Economies of scale.
World phase (1980s)	• Top quality AND low cost becomes the baseline. • Competitive advantage comes from strategic thinking, mass customization, and outlearning competitors. • Mass production with small adaptation to local markets at the end of the value chain allows keeping cost down while pleasing local markets at global scale. • The concept of "glocalization" (think global, act local), is born.
Decentralized phase (2000)	• Stabilization and enhancement of large production blocks. • Definition of pre-industrialized/industrialized and post-industrialized countries. • Sensitivity to ecological matters. • Cross-cultural thinking in design as a productivity enhancer.
Networked phase (2020)	• Knowledge-based society meets production needs. • Project-based operations led by networks of SMEs. • Quick reactions, first move players, creativity, and innovation. • Research-focused approach. • Knowledge-based networks.

The different stages in the globalization process have affected cross-cultural management differently and different cultures have faced this phenomenon in very different ways, according to their own characteristics and socially developed tools to face the issues relating to changes in ways of working and the evolution of international trade.

As an example of the previous statements, we can quote another Wikipedia entry, which also quotes an interesting point of view relating to globalization.

Finally, Takis Fotopoulos argues that globalization is the result of systemic trends manifesting the market economy's grow-or-die dynamic, following the rapid expansion of transnational corporations. Because these trends have not been offset effectively by counter-tendencies that could have emanated from trade-union action and other forms of political activity, the outcome has been globalization. This is a multi-faceted and irreversible phenomenon within the system of the market economy and it is expressed as: economic globalization, namely, the opening and deregulation of commodity, capital and labor markets which led to the present form of neoliberal globalization; political globalization, i.e., the emergence of a transnational elite and the phasing out of the all of the statist period; cultural globalization, i.e., the worldwide homogenization of culture; ideological globalization; technological globalization; social globalization.

The different phases in the globalization process have impacted cultures involved in the process in many ways. Whereas in the domestic phase, dealing internationally consisted basically in speaking a common language at least basically or communicating through translators on very specific and objective matters (i.e., prices, delivery options, conditions, contract clauses), other phases have required the enhancement of a more evolved communication arena.

For instance, in the multilocal phase, some companies decided to delegate responsibility for the operations to local managers (this was the preferred American style), and these agents also operated as the interface between headquarters and the subsidiaries, absorbing most of the cross-cultural biases and disruptions. Other companies (in general this was the preferred French style) sent expatriates to deal with local uses and operational standards, bearing in mind that the general practice designed at headquarters was the one to be put into practice at local level. In any case, each subsidiary would very much act local and also think local and headquarters would not mind very much about specifications or ways of doing things abroad, as long as the financial objectives were met. The impact of globalization on society up to this stage was not very important, as it implied little work mobility and no change in production processes or management procedures.

It was probably during the multinational phase that globalization produced the strongest impact on societies, as the production patterns were applied universally, but designed from headquarters. Companies started producing gains that allowed them to expand without borders and enhance their overall power and governmental lobby capacity as never seen before. Many consumer products were standardized and consumed in similar manners across the globe and labor was hired where it was cheaper, not always considering the impact of this choice on local welfare or even sometimes human rights (i.e., child labor was employed, health and safety conditions of employees were often not respected, etc.).

During the global phase, quality became an issue, imposing new regulations on international producers. Even if the international consumers felt tempted by the cheaper products during the first stages of globalization, soon they became disappointed by the poor quality of what they bought and this reality gave a new kick to local small manufacturers. Once the globalization process was perfected, numerous SMEs across the globe disappeared, remaining unable to compete with the giants, causing unemployment.

The problems that arose with globalization during the first phases, in particular during the multinational phase mostly concerned under-developed and developing nations. The most recent stages, nevertheless, mainly affect the most developed countries. The decentralized and the networked phases of globalization brought with them the need to exploit the brainpower of nations to their maximum in order to generate and support the knowledge based society. In this sense, as the manual operations are executed in specific locations, leaving the high added value activities to concentrate in headquarters (postindustrialized countries), there was a two-way flow of population: unqualified workers received incentives to move to destinations where the factories were, and at the same time, qualified brains were welcomed by postindustrialized nations, who wanted to attract those able to perform high added-value tasks.

The networked phase, though, because of its location independent characteristics, does not call for the physical presence of the workers where they perform their professional tasks, and therefore should reduce the amount of migration through different methods. Strategically positioned networks concentrate brainpower in locations worldwide and these units interact on short-term projects worldwide. Even if the networked phase mostly concerns qualified workers, this arrangement will probably equally concern the less-qualified portion of the population, as developments in technology will progressively allow the replacement of routine jobs currently done by men, by machines.

The new landscape beyond 2010 will probably be designed by networks, which as predicted will act beyond national borders and the ruling class will probably be the most qualified and powerful, or at least the one that would have accessed knowledge and know-how to the point of becoming indispensable for the networks.

Many have wondered whether globalization would destroy multiculturalism and the answer to that question cannot easily be found. Some authors like Geert Hofstede may state that globalization can only affect practices (the way we do things), but not values and therefore the inception of new products and techniques would only have a limited impact on culture. On the other side, mobility will be enhanced and networks will be established, which would indicate that probably culture would be more affected by the fact that one belongs to a network or not, rather than by nationality.

Multicultural regions like the EU are trying very hard to find a common denominator in order to develop a common sense of belonging across member states with varied levels of success. On one side, the Christian tradition was intended to be a strong linking factor, but the incorporation of Turkey within the block would strongly challenge this fact. Perhaps it is the idea of a common future together that would link countries, or the facilitated internal mobility could at some point generate a powerful sense of unity. Whether this unity will ever mean the loss of identity is arguable.

Pressure groups have wanted to limit the extension of the impact of globalization, but the phenomenon is just unavoidable: for as long as technology is put in hand to disseminate ways and uses, globalization will continue to expand. In any case, nations have been subject to the invasion of other cultures for centuries and they are in fact the result of the conjunction between the old and the new—whether the "new" is imposed or just voluntarily acquired. Just as an example (amongst thousands of others), no matter how unified, unique and ethnically homogeneous a nation like France could seem, it is just the result of the conjunction of a huge number of cultures that have occupied its current territory through the centuries: Romans, Celtics, Germanics, Vikings, Gauls, Normans, and so on have contributed to change and to stability and to what we know today as France.

Perhaps what is essentially different since the big impact of globalization has started to take place is the way in which change is absorbed. Until now, the incorporation of new uses and costumes was confined to the specific geographic territory in which it took place (i.e., the Romans invade Gaul and then the Gaul discovers pizza), but the new practices did not go beyond each geographic confinement individually. Contrary to that, nowadays incoming factors (inventions, technology, Facebook, iPads, etc.) affect the globe in its entirety at once, on the spot and at the same time and in the same way and therefore evolution tends in many ways towards the same uses and customs, or at least to the same practices across the world, at the same time, as if a huge force was invading the planet as a whole.

This very particular aspect of the way in which change in cultures takes place due to technological progress (which recognizes no land borders) has led and continues to lead to two very specific and very particular characteristics of current times: (1) culture will increasingly develop in terms of subcultures and less in terms of national cultures and (2) the big social and economic differences will not be geographical, but knowledge-based.

The first effects of these changes are visible already: for instance, changes in education start to occur. Traditionally in most countries primary school education was in many ways a preparation for war: from the study of national anthems and other battlefield songs to the presentation of the glory of the nation through the victories of its heroes, children from almost every country were taught that they were part of a group to which they owed loyalty in exchange for protection. Most of us have been brought up that way. A more creativity-enhancing, free-thinking, culturally friendly, nonracist education is being generated in order to respond to the new needs of the world, which tends towards an innovation-led paradigm as opposed to a field-owning regime which might at some stage and with little anticipation call for the blood of youngsters to defend the common property.

In the old days in which immigration only took place gradually, it was easier to recognize foreigners: in many cases they looked different. It was easy to create stereotypes, to judge and to set areas of the population apart.

As the world develops towards innovation and the knowledge based society, the differences that used to be visible become unreliable: nations are multi-racial and in order to attract the best brains from wherever they come from, the way a person looks will less and less be considered as a reliable indicator of his/her position in society, his/her wealth, or his/her background.

For years and years, the notion of "security" has been strongly linked to that of "nationality" or "inhabiting a land." Most basic rights are acquired through a nationality. Our nation's reason to exist is that it provides safety and security, plus a sense of belonging to those constituting it. This is part of the social contract that we have been socialized upon. Within the new circumstances, with networks assuming the role of job providers and status warrantors, the fact is not so certain any longer. Some nations (the UK for instance), start publishing brochures in which they mention a new concept "one needs to **deserve** to be a citizen"... this implies a huge change in the collective mental programming. People do not just "obtain" a nationality, they need to actually be worthy of it.

Terrorism has somehow contributed to change in mental programming. The "enemy" might be within us. At first, terrorism was linked to Muslim extremists, radicalists, or specific groups outside civilized society. Until recently, criminal acts were countered by nationalism, which would correspond to the traditional reaction of land versus enemy (i.e., the United States versus Bin Laden). But since terrorism is now becoming the action of individuals **within** society (i.e., Anders Behring Breivik's mass murder in Norway), the old ways of patriotically aligning against the common foreign enemy seem to have lost their efficacy. And other forms of security impose themselves (socially accepted technological espionage being one of them).

When living in conditions in which change is happening faster than we can realize, where parameters are evolving at such a rate that we cannot follow, and at times where everything we had always considered as true, may simply be not so any longer, societies need to adapt and mentalities need to change.

Nations will probably not define us and protect us for much longer to the same extent as they used to. Having lived on a piece of land for many genera-tions may no longer guarantee safety, security, or even identity. Identities may need to be self-constructed to a higher extent and it might become necessary to work to deserve to be part of a group that provides for some of our needs.

So, how will humanity satisfy its own need for identification, social belonging, and interaction with peers? For years, the main socialization factor was belonging to a culture, a country, a region, and so forth, and identity was made visible through symbols and external materialization of them. Globalization has an important influence in turning most of these symbols into anecdotal picturesque objects that remind us more of the history of a place than of the history of people themselves.

We find ourselves at present in the midst of a transition from a situation in which nation states provide safety and security, identity, and status; to a new one in which all these assets are to be merited and the networks to which one is linked to determine each one's position in society (which is borderless) and grant the sense of belonging. Safety and security does not come from solidarity towards those who share the same nationality, but from the fact that our lives become visible to everyone through the information we volunteer through our computer at every moment.

The transition is harsh to go through, as it leaves us frozen in front of a new framework of mind to adapt to and to operate from.

In this sense, collective cultures may need to alter their criteria of connections in order to adapt them to the networks that will determine the new social ruling; masculine societies will have to recognize that in order to support the new ways of production gender can no longer be a barrier if we are to maximize the use of the brainpower that exists in each block; internal locus of control cultures will need to depart from their need to adapt to the unknown, rather than mastering it; synchronic cultures will need to focus on the future, rather than on the past; status will be more achieved than ascribed; power distance will be shorter and emotionals will need to control how they express themselves, as information that is put online will remain on record forever.

Using This Information

To reflect and get ready for the years to come!

Discussion Point

Now review the following statements and comment on them. What do they mean? Who could have said them?

- "Think global, act local"
- "The doctrine of free trade, if applied globally, will be a disaster"
- "Economies should not be self-serving structures, but directed at promoting the stability and contentment of the societies within which they operate"
- "Europe faces a future of unemployment, poverty and social instability"
- "Britain will become the Mexico of Europe"
- "A reason for this is our quasi-religious belief in free trade. A moral dogma which was born when Britain was the manufacturing centre of the world"
- "A world of fence-off regions with economies that reflect local conditions, cultures and needs"

Get Into Globalens.com

Go to the www.globalens.com web page and access the following cases:

- Detroit Motors and General Auto: A Case Study in Globalization, Outsourcing and Automation
- Western Union: A Case for Global Expansion
- Globalization Comes to Nakamura Lacquer Company
- Jim Thompson Thai Silk Company
- NAFTA Arrives at Maxwell Tomato Farms
- Vostok Watches

Now compare the previously listed cases of companies entering the globalization process and determine in which aspects they were successful and in which they were not. What are common issues that appear in all cases? What are particular/industry specific matters?

Prepare a comparative table like the one below and then elaborate in writing.

Issue	Detroit	Western Union	Nakamura	Maxwell	Vostok	Another company of your choice
Adaptation to new tastes						
Problems with employees						
Different demands from different markets						
Etc.						
Etc.						
Etc.						

Notes

Chapter 1

1. Hofstede (1984).
2. House, Hanges, Javidan, Dorfman, and Gupta (2004).
3. Bollinger and Hofstede (1987).
4. Al-Aiban and Pearce (1995).

Chapter 2

1. Hofstede, Hofstede, and Minkov (2010).

Chapter 3

1. Trompenaars and Hampden-Turner (1997).
2. Julian Rotter is an American psychologist, born in 1916. He developed the social learning theory and also established a bridge between behaviorism and cognitive psychology.
3. Hall (1988).

Chapter 4

1. Schein (2010).
2. Trompenaars and Hampden-Turner (1997).
3. Strodtbeck and Kluckhohn (1961).
4. Adler (2010).
5. Hall (1988).
6. Hofstede (1984).
7. Katan (1999).
8. Used by permission of Gregory A. Bissky, from Treasure Mountain Consultants.
9. Milgram (1994).

Chapter 5

1. Edgar Henry Schein (b. 1928), a professor at the MIT Sloan School of Management, has made a notable mark in the field of organizational development

in many areas, including career development, group process consultation, and organizational culture. He is generally credited with inventing the term "corporate culture." (The *Oxford English Dictionary* traces the phrase "corporate culture" as far back as 1966. *Academy of Management Journal 9*, 362/2.) Source: *Wikipedia.*
2. Hunsaker and Cook (1986).
3. Hofstede (1999).
4. d'Iribarne (1993).

Chapter 6

1. Moran, Harris, and Moran (2007).
2. Berlo (1960).
3. Adler (2008).
4. Source: *Wikipedia.* http://en.wikipedia.org/wiki/List_of_languages_by_number_of_native_speakers
5. Mehrabian (2009).
6. Noller (1984).
7. Hall (1966).
8. Gudykunst (2004).

Chapter 7

1. Ghauri and Usunier (2003).
2. Hofstede (1999).

Chapter 8

1. Hellriegel, Slocum, and Woodman (2001).
2. Gladwin and Walter (1980).

Chapter 10

1. Machiavelli (2011).
2. Friedman (2002).
3. Ryan (2000).

4. Mill (2004).
5. Kant (2007).
6. Allinson (1995); Trevino and Nelson (1995); Marcic (1997) in Linstead et al. (2004).
7. Donaldson and Dunfee (1999).

Chapter 11

1. Hill (1994).

Chapter 12

1. Adler and Gundersen (2007).

References

Adler, A. (2010). *Understanding human nature*. Mansfield Center, CT: Martino Publishing.

Adler, N. J. (2008). *International dimensions of organizational behavior* (5th ed.). Mason, USA: Thomason, South-Western.

Adler, N. J., & Gundersen, A. (2007). *International dimensions of organizational behavior* (5th Revised ed.). Cincinnati, OH: South Western College.

Al-Aiban, K. M., & Pearce, J. L. (1995). The influence of values on management practices. *International Studies of Management & Organization 23*(3), 35–52.

Berlo, D. K. (1960). *The process of communication*. New York: Holt, Rinehart & Winston.

Bollinger, D., & Hofstede, G. (1987). *Les differences culturelles dans le management: comment chaque pays gere-t-il ses hommes?* Paris, France: Editions de l'Organisation.

Donaldson, T., & Dunfee, T. (1999). *Ties that bind: A social contracts approach to business ethics*. Cambridge, MA: Harvard Business School Press.

Friedman, M. (2002). *Capitalism and freedom* (40th Anniversary ed.). Chicago, IL: University of Chicago Press.

Ghauri, P. N., & Usunier, J.-C. (2003). *International business negotiations* (2nd ed.; International Business and Management). Bingley, UK: Emerald.

Gladwin, T. N. & Walter, I. (1980). *Multinationals under fire: lessons in the management of conflict*. New York, NY: John Wiley & Sons Inc.

Gudykunst, W. B. (2004). *Bridging differences—effective intergroup communication* (4th ed.). Thousand Oaks, CA: Sage Publications, Inc.

Hall, E. (1966). *The hidden dimension*. New York, NY: Anchor Books.

Hall, E. (1988, July 1). *Silent language* (Reissue ed.). New York, NY: Bantam Doubleday Dell Publishing Group.

Hellriegel, D., Slocum, J., & Woodman, R. (2001). *Organizational behaviour* (9th ed.; p. 294). Cincinnati, OH: South-Western College Publishing, Thomson Learning.

Hill, L. (1994, March 5). Managing your team. *Harvard Business Review*. Case Number: 494081.

Hofstede, G. (1984). *Culture's consequences*. California, USA: Sage publications.

Hofstede, G. (1999). Problems remain, but theories will change: The universal and the specific in 21st-century global management. *Organizational Dynamics 28*(1), 34–44.

Hofstede, G., Hofstede, G. J., & Minkov, M. (2010, June 1). *Cultures and organizations: Software for the mind* (3rd ed.; Intercultural Cooperation and Its Importance for Survival). New York, USA: McGraw-Hill Professional.

House, R. J., Hanges, P. J., Javidan, M., Dorfman, P. W., & Gupta, V. (2004). *Culture, leadership, and organizations: The Globe Study of 62 societies* (eds.). Thousand Oaks, CA: Sage.

Hunsaker, P., & Cook, C. (1986). *Managing organisational behaviour*. Reading, MA: Addison-Wesley.

d'Iribarne, P. (1993). *La logique de l'honneur—Gestion des entreprises et traditions nationals*. Paris: Seuil.

Kant, I. (2007). *Critique of pure reason* (Penguin Classics; Rev ed.). London: Penguin.

Katan, D. (1999). *Translating cultures: An introduction for translators, interpreters, and mediators*. Manchester: St. Jerome Publishing.

Linstead, S., Fulop, L., & Lilley, S. (2004). *Management and organization*. London: Palgrave.

Machiavelli, N. (2011). *The prince* (Special Student ed.). Retrieved from: http://www.amazon.com/Prince-Special-Student-Niccolo-Machiavelli/dp/1936594455/ref=sr_1_11?s=books&ie=UTF8&qid=1315439888&sr=1–11

Mehrabian, A. (2009). "Silent messages"—A wealth of information about nonverbal communication (body language). *Personality & Emotion Tests & Software: Psychological Books & Articles of Popular Interest*. Los Angeles, CA: Self-published. Retrieved April 6, 2010.

Milgram, S. (1994). *Soumission a l'autorité*. Paris: Calmann-Lévy.

Mill, J. (2004). *Utilitarianism*. Public Domain Books.

Moran, R. T., Harris, P. R., & Moran, S. V. (2007). *Managing cultural differences: Global leadership strategies for the twenty-first century* (7th ed.). Burlington, MA: Butterworth-Heinemann.

Noller, P. (1984). *Nonverbal communication and marital interaction*. Oxford, UK: Pergamon.

Ryan, A. (ed.) (2000). *John Stuart Mill and Jeremy Bentham: Utilitarianism and other essays* (Penguin Classics) (1st ed.). London: Pearson Education.

Schein, E. H. (2010, August 27). *Organizational culture and leadership* (The Jossey-Bass Business & Management Series; 4th ed.). San Francisco, CA: Jossey Bass.

Strodtbeck, F., & Kluckhohn, L. (1961). *Variations in value orientations*. New York, NY: Row, Peterson and Company.

Trompenaars, F., & Hampden-Turner, C. (1997, September 15). *Riding the waves of culture: Understanding cultural diversity in* business (2nd Revised ed.). New York, USA: Nicholas Brealey Publishing.

Index

Announcing the Business Expert Press Digital Library

Concise E-books Business Students Need for Classroom and Research

This book can also be purchased in an e-book collection by your library as

- a one-time purchase,
- that is owned forever,
- allows for simultaneous readers,
- has no restrictions on printing, and
- can be downloaded as PDFs from within the library community.

Our digital library collections are a great solution to beat the rising cost of textbooks. e-books can be loaded into their course management systems or onto student's e-book readers.

The **Business Expert Press** digital libraries are very affordable, with no obligation to buy in future years.

For more information, please visit **www.businessexpertpress.com/librarians**.

To set up a trial in the United States, please contact **Sheri Dean** at *sheri.dean@globalepress.com*; for all other regions, contact **Nicole Lee** at *nicole.lee@igroupnet.com*.

OTHER TITLES IN OUR HUMAN RESOURCE MANAGEMENT AND ORGANIZATIONAL BEHAVIOR COLLECTION

Collection Editors: **Stan Gully and Jean Phillips**, *Rutgers*

Career Management by Vijay Sathe

Developing Employee Talent to Perform by Kim Warren

Conducting Performance Appraisals by Michael Gordon and Vernon Miller

Culturally Intelligent Leadership: Leading Through Intercultural Interactions by Mai Moua

Letting People Go: The People-Centered Approach to Firing and Laying Off Employees by Matt Shlosberg

The Five Golden Rules of Negotiation by Philippe Korda

CPSIA information can be obtained at www.ICGtesting.com
Printed in the USA
BVOW030743121211

278113BV00006B/1/P